# How to Build
# a Business

## and Sell It for Millions

# How to Build
# a Business

## and Sell It for Millions

Jack Garson

St. Martin's Press ⋙ New York

This information provided in this book is for informational purposes only and is not legal, financial, or other professional advice. You should consult with professional advisors regarding the specific facts and circumstances of your situation. In addition, except for references to actual companies that are identified by name, the author has changed identifying information regarding the real people and organizations that inspired the lessons that follow. In many instances important details are changed and/or composites of multiple cases are used to illustrate the author's points.

HOW TO BUILD A BUSINESS AND SELL IT FOR MILLIONS. Copyright © 2010 by Jack Garson. All rights reserved. Printed in the United States of America. For information, address St. Martin's Press, 175 Fifth Avenue, New York, N.Y. 10010.

www.stmartins.com

Design by Level C

ISBN 978-0-312-38311-4

First Edition: March 2010

10  9  8  7  6  5  4  3  2  1

# Dedication

To Phil Revzin and the rest of the St. Martin's team, who gave me this opportunity and helped me make the most of it,

To my parents, who taught me right from wrong,

To Alison Coombs, my trusty aide, who laughs at my jokes and fixes my mistakes,

To my partner, Rick Claxton, and the rest of my colleagues at Garson Claxton for their integrity, service, and excellence,

To Marc Silverstein, media whiz, who pushed and guided me to do my best work,

To my wife, Marcy Lynn, who, since our first date on Valentine's Day 1986, has always believed in me,

To all the successful entrepreneurs who showed me how it's done,

My heartfelt thanks and everlasting gratitude.

# Contents

# Introduction

I'll never forget the call.

"The deal is dead."

The deal team had been working day and night for six months to sell Bobby's company. Tens of millions of dollars were on the table. We had started with grueling all-day negotiations that seemed to never end, arguing over the major economic and legal terms and the wording of countless provisions of a 100-plus-page contract. Then we gathered and studied a war room full of agreements that representatives of the company had signed over the last decade and countless other documents that we had to give the buyer. Next, we were on the phone with the buyer's due-diligence consultants answering endless questions. We ran all over town getting third-party opinions and pulling copies of licenses, permits, and government certificates. Remember the last time you went to the motor vehicle bureau to get your driver's license renewed? Well, try renewing the driver's licenses for everyone in the state, on the last day of a hot August, during the staff's lunch break. It was just like that, but without the air-conditioning. We answered more questions and provided still more due-diligence materials and then endured the purchaser's renegotiation of several major terms. Finally, we thought we were done. Oh, we were done all right, but not in a good way.

"Dead?"

"Yes," said the opposing counsel.

That was it. Over. Done. Go home early tonight and the next night. Oh, sure, the purchaser gave us their reasons, and, frankly, they were no surprise. Our seller, Bobby, had no executive team—no "bench strength." He ran a company with tens of millions in sales and was the only senior executive. The company was the "Bobby show." If Bobby got hit by a bus, the company would be out of business in weeks, maybe months with some luck. Also, Bobby had no sophisticated financial systems. The company had a bookkeeper masquerading as a Chief Financial Officer. We couldn't produce a monthly statement on time and the annual statements bore little resemblance to a modern-day Balance Sheet and Operating Statement. Forget Generally Accepted Accounting Principles—hell, Bobby's CFO thought GAAP was the distance between the loading dock and one of their trucks. Try paper accounting books and pencil entries. No kidding. That's the business we were stuck trying to sell. Once the purchaser dug in, the purchaser realized that it was about to buy a company with good revenues and profits but doubtful "scalability" (the ability to grow the company) and questionable "sustainability" (the ability to survive disasters).

It's not that I hadn't warned Bobby. On the contrary, I beat the drum on both of these issues for years. The simple fact was that Bobby was trapped in the classic Founder's Dilemma. What made him fantastic in starting the business now held him back in growing it. Bobby exemplified the pull-yourself-up-by-your-bootstraps entrepreneur. For over a decade, he worked twelve or more hours per day. He managed, maybe micromanaged, every aspect of the business to keep his costs down, to keep customers happy, to keep sales coming in, and to maintain the quality of his services. That's how he built what was now a business with sales ramping up every year and profit margins that grew even more.

So my advice had fallen on deaf ears when I told Bobby to hire expensive executives to take over various parts of his business and invest in costly, but necessary, accounting and financial systems.

Then again, when our deal to sell the company died, so did Bobby's dream of time with his kids before they got too old and a big house on a hill and seeing a little bit of the world. Bobby was weary and finally willing to hear some often-repeated "new" ideas. We brought on a President for the company who had been a division leader with a Fortune 100 company. We promoted Bobby to CEO. We also added a VP of sales and a sales team. We hired a real CFO straight out of what was then one of the Big 6 accounting firms. The CFO scrapped the abacuses and slide rules and put in a bona fide accounting system. The VP of sales and his team began the process of bonding the customers to the company instead of Bobby's charm, thereby "institutionalizing" the customer base in a way that would be of greater value to any purchaser of the company. The new President, a man of wisdom, foresight, and finesse, and a few gray hairs to boot, began the process of creating a company that would not merely survive Bobby's ultimate—and desired—departure but also thrive. Although, up close, it did appear as if Bobby had a tear or two in his eyes when the company's payroll jumped up those first few months.

But now we had what every sophisticated purchaser would want. Not just a profitable company. We had the scalability to grow the company—and justify the price that Bobby would require to sell it. And we had the sustainability to thrive despite difficult times and Bobby's imminent retirement.

The second time around, the deal didn't die. Sales were bumping up around $100 million annually, profit margins continued to increase, and the new executive team and financial systems were in place. We didn't just sell the company. We held an auction. Working with one of the best investment bankers on the eastern seaboard, we lined up six prospective purchasers, all of whom were eager to throw their money at us. We did our own due diligence and weeded them down to three finalists, all motivated to make a deal. We required the finalists to resubmit revised "best and final offers." This step alone increased the sales price for the company by $10 million.

We picked the best candidate from among the finalists and began negotiating the terms of a letter of intent (LOI). We avoided the amateur mistake of agreeing to negotiate exclusively with this party for an unduly long time period. The short negotiating period meant that if the prospective buyer tried to "retrade"—or renegotiate—the deal, we could still do a deal with the other prospects before they had moved on to different deals. Also, we avoided the purchaser's typical insistence that the sales price was capped in the LOI and could go down if revenues slipped; such a one-sided provision undermines the buyer's motivation to move quickly. Instead, we prompted the buyer to move quickly by using a formula that would increase the sales price as our sales and profits increased.

The lessons learned from the past paid incredible dividends. We had turned our weaknesses into strengths. We sold the company not merely based on our sales and profits but also based on leadership and systems that could grow the company after Bobby's departure.

Fifteen years earlier, Bobby had started a small company with a trade secret and a partner. The trade secret was better than the partner. Bobby bought out the partner early on and always believed in himself and his vision. Yet Bobby never ever imagined that he could build a business with $100 million in revenues and then sell it. Frankly, he didn't know how. Now, years later, with a lot of hard work and the right guidance, Bobby did it. After paying off company debt, distributing bonuses, and paying taxes, Bobby netted $60 million. And it wasn't brain surgery or rocket science. In fact, it's all here in this book.

# How to Build
# a Business
## and Sell It for Millions

# 1

# Planning to Sell

## *Putting the Horse in Front of the Cart*

Amerca has hunkered down. People have cut back wherever they can. Folks are brown-bagging lunch—if they still have a job. They're cutting their own lawns and one another's hair. Families take in-home "staycations" instead of trips to Disneyland.

Your moment has arrived.

You may have always wanted to start your own company. You may have just gotten fired and have no other choice but to go into business for yourself. You may have a business that isn't growing and needs fixing.

Perfect timing.

Building and selling your own business has always been one of the greatest paths to wealth. Now it's the opportunity of a lifetime. This is the best time in decades to plunge in. As the economy revives there will be pent-up demand for what businesses have to sell. Better still, people with briefcases full of money will be clamoring to buy those businesses.

But it's not enough to build your business now and worry about selling it later. From day one, you need to know what buyers want to buy and then create it. You shouldn't knock yourself out for years building a business only to discover you can't sell it. Planning to sell—from that very first day—is putting the horse in front of the cart.

## The Coming Boom:
## Making Your Fortune in Business

The next big thing in business is starting your own company, building it up, and selling it for a bundle. When real estate crumbled in the early 1990s, investors ultimately turned to technology companies and created the dot-com boom. When that boom went crash, investors renewed their love affair with real estate—and thus was born *condomania*. It felt like there were more construction cranes in Miami and Las Vegas than tourists. Now stocks and real estate have plunged once again. Battered investors are not about to fall madly in love with either of them for a while. Personally, I'd rule out comic books, baseball cards, and Beanie Babies, too.

Making money the old-fashioned way, by starting a business, growing it like crazy, and then cashing out, is about to come back into style.

If you're wondering if the timing is right, consider this: At this writing we are in the worst recession since the Great Depression. Throughout history, though, some of the most successful businesses were created in the most difficult of times. General Electric was formed by Thomas Edison during the six-year recession called the Panic of 1873. Disney began business in the recession of 1923–24. Hewlett-Packard was started at the end of the Great Depression. It only stands to reason that a company that succeeds in dire circumstances—when so many others fail—will thrive in normal times and excel in boom times.

Now consider the buyers of businesses. In recessions, they conserve cash and maybe even run out of it. Certainly they get cautious. So they slow down and even stop buying businesses. Coming out of a recession, they're looking for steals. They start buying companies again—but just the best businesses and only at bargain prices. Buyers make a killing off those early deals. Then, pumped up by those lucrative returns, they broadcast their success to attract acclaim and investors. Thus the gold rush begins. Other buyers stampede onto the scene, looking to strike it rich buying companies.

The business sales in the next few years will bring on a mad dash of buyers and deals that get better and better for sellers. If you start now, you'll be in a position to sell at an extraordinary time.

## Planning to Sell

Planning to sell is all about building—from the very start—a business that people want to buy. The folks who purchase companies don't want a business where every customer asks for you and you're long gone. They certainly don't want a business that, as harsh as it sounds, dies with you. They want an enduring institution, a reliable moneymaking machine that will grow and last.

Of course, you don't *need* to build up your business or sell it. You can run your business so that it meets your everyday desires, whether that means golf every afternoon and poker every night or just enough money for Cheez-Its, lottery tickets, and cable television. They even have a name for that type of business—a "lifestyle business," because it prioritizes your lifestyle over your company. You can run your business like a hobby. You can live a decent life as chief bottle washer and cook. You can even put a bullet in your business when you retire. Life is full of choices.

But to get all of the possible value out of your business—to increase the chance you'll achieve enormous wealth—you need to build something that you can sell. You need to create something that buyers compete to buy.

Buyers look for a lot of things, but at the very top of the list are the following:

**PROFITABILITY:** A business that consistently makes money. Ideally your profits increase every year.

**COMPETITIVE EDGE:** A business that beats the competition. Face it: once you're making money, you'll attract rivals. Buyers want to make sure that competitors can't duplicate your success or cut into your profits.

**SCALABILITY:** A business that can grow bigger. Buyers want to increase the size, revenues, and profits of your company. The decisions you make from the outset, from how you form your company, to the equipment you buy, to the brand you establish, all affect "scalability"—the future ability to grow your business. If you want to sell for big bucks, you need a company that can get big.

**SUSTAINABILITY:** A business that can make it through adversity. You may not have enough capital. You may not back up your computers. You may not even have employees who can do your job if you get sick. But if your company can't withstand a few disasters, you'll never be in a position to survive, much less sell. Buyers don't want a company that tumbles like a house of cards in the first heavy breeze. They're only going to pay a lot if you've built a company that can make it through tough times.

There's more. There's picking the right legal structure for your business, creating financial systems so you can manage your business, avoiding unnecessary risks, preparing good contracts, marketing, government relations—and more. There's learning the way businesses are sold, how to assemble the deal team to sell your company, and how to negotiate the sale itself—and more.

Building a business, overcoming problems, and selling your company present countless challenges. But you don't have to do it the hard way.

## The Easy Hard Way

I've seen sweat on the foreheads of great business leaders struggling with momentous decisions. I've sat in thousands of boardrooms and business meetings where entrepreneurs agonized over issues that would determine the fate of their companies. I've seen their responses yield victories and defeats. In the lessons that follow, you'll see and learn from their successes and failures.

With the guidance in this book you can learn how to build a business that sells. This is the insider's guide to what works and what doesn't—what you need and what you need to avoid. Selling a business can be hard. But it's not hard to sell a good business.

# 2

# Profitable Business Model

*Making Money Every Time*

A lex took the road less traveled. He was the only one of my old college buddies who struck out on his own after graduation. The rest of us went the tried-and-true method, landing jobs in corporate America. Boy, did we think we had it made. For the first time we had money in our pockets, wore nice suits, bought new cars and town houses, got married, and started down a well-worn path toward forty years of working for The Man. Alex, on the other hand, always looked like he just rolled out of bed, never shaved, wore ripped jeans and old sweatshirts, and drove a beat-up old Corvair that puffed out big blue clouds of burning oil.

But Alex had a plan. Not just any plan. He had a business plan.

Alex wanted to dot highways running through the countryside with dozens of billboards. He saw dollar signs because a new law banned most highway signs. New billboards would be scarce but all that much more valuable to advertisers. Alex's plan: Find locations. Lease them. Build billboards. Sell ads. Open bank account. Deposit advertisers' checks.

Early on we thought Alex and his plan were crazy. We had visions of tromping out in the fields, building billboards, and gluing up ads. You might as well have tried talking us into becoming garbagemen. No one at the country club was going to be bragging about their son the billboard mogul. We all thought Alex was crazy, until we saw how much money he was making. By then, there were only two things we could do: overcome our envy and someday include Alex's plan in a book. I've only managed to accomplish the latter.

## Successful Business Plans and Profitable Business Models

Unlike the plans of so many hopeful entrepreneurs, Alex's plan made money. In business terms, he had a (1) *successful business plan*, which, when properly implemented, produced a (2) *profitable business model*.

These two concepts are often intertwined, but it is important to understand the connection and the differences. Here's a simple analogy to help you better understand these terms.

Business Plan = Blueprint.

Business Model = House.

If the blueprint (business plan) is good, the house (business model) will have every room and amenity you want, won't cost a fortune to build or maintain, and will be easy and profitable to sell.

Alex took his blueprint (his plan) and built a billboard empire (the model). Armed with his homemade map and knowledge of the laws, Alex knew exactly where to go. A bunch of farmers owned land in the right locations. They didn't take to shiny-shoed city types. Fortunately, Alex wasn't. Unshaven and unpretentious, he charmed them with his genuine "aw shucks, I'm just a hardworking kid." The farmers warmed to him. Eventually, they agreed to let Alex lease small slivers of their land and install billboards. It didn't cost much to put up each billboard, maybe a few thousand dollars. Then the advertisers, starved for outdoor locations, eagerly paid thousands of dollars per month for each of Alex's choice spots. The revenue from each billboard paid for all the start-up costs in just a few months. After that, the business generated thousands of dollars per month in profits from each and every billboard.

So what happened here? Alex had a business that made a lot of money and would make more as each year passed. His competitors couldn't do much to change that, because he had airtight agreements that locked up key pieces of land for many years. And the advertisers weren't going away. They would always want locations where thousands of people in passing cars could see their messages. Best of all, there would be plenty of people eager to buy Alex's business. Why not? It made money. It made more money as each year passed. It would make money in good times and bad.

## Starting with a Business Plan

A good business plan sounds basic, but it's difficult to achieve. Here's why. Get out a pencil and list every significant thing you need for your business—whether it's labor, raw materials, brainpower, trucks, a store, a phone system and other equipment, or anything else. List where you're going to get it all from and what it will cost. The following is just a warm-up, but you're going to have to figure out answers to challenging questions like these:

- Will anything change in the next week, next month, or next year that affects the availability of these items and, if so, what is your contingency plan for an alternative source?

- Will those changes alter your costs?

- Who are your potential customers?

- How will you let them know you exist and how you will sell to them?

- How will you price your goods and services?

- How are your competitors pricing similar goods and services?

- Will your competitors drive prices down and push you from a profit to a loss?

- Why will customers buy from you instead of your competitors?

- Why will customers buy from you again, the second day you're in business?

Did that scare you? I hope you now understand why it's difficult to actually make money, especially on a consistent basis.

Why ask these questions? Because it's a valuable drill. You need to make sure you have a business plan that will produce a profitable business model. If, continuing with our "house" analogy, your blueprint produces a house with a leaky roof, mold, and endless repairs, you have a bad plan. You want a plan that produces a house that you'll enjoy year after year and be able to sell for a profit.

## Fads Versus Business Models

Keep in mind that a profitable business model not only requires your revenues to consistently exceed your expenses but also has to work over time and throughout various business cycles. As so many dot-commers discovered, it's not a profitable business model if you start with a lot of invested money and never reliably sell your products for a profit. Day traders and real estate speculators eventually realize that "flipping" is not a profitable business model if you only make money for a limited time period or under unique circumstances. It's certainly not a profitable business model if you're a contractor taking the deposit from your latest job to satisfy the bill collectors from your last project. Mind you, you may be able to make a quick profit from even the shakiest of business models. But it won't produce profits year after year and you're not going to get rich selling your business. The people who have enough money to pay tens and hundreds of millions of dollars for a company don't usually hand over all that money unless your business is a real winner.

## Disastrous Ideas and Bad Plans

When it comes to business plans, don't confuse an *"Attaboy!"* with a business model. Just because your brother lets you cut his hair doesn't mean you should cash in your 401(k) and open a salon. Repeat after me: just because everyone in your family loves your lasagna doesn't mean you should take that inheritance and open a restaurant. Again: just because you found a way to duct-tape the handle so the toilet doesn't run all night doesn't mean you should mortgage the house to set up a plumbing shop.

I can't even count how many would-be entrepreneurs I've sat down who didn't have a good business plan. They might have an idea or a dream or a fantasy, but they didn't have a plan. I hear it every day: ideas like Cat TV, where a client wanted to put dials and knobs on aquariums so cats can "watch fish on TV." It just says bankruptcy! A roadside coffee stand was another one, which *might* work great during rush hours, assuming not too many of your customers get run over. Recently someone suggested to me the idea of holding wine tours on a blimp. Have you ever been on a blimp? They're loud and cramped and the novelty wears off quickly. Also, drinking copious amounts of intoxicating beverages and swaying in the air has a peculiar effect on some people. Watch out below!

Other people have a plan—a *bad* plan. I ask them, "If you do everything according to your plan, will this business make money?" Blank stares. Sometimes tears. Most can't answer. At the end of the day, they don't know if they will make money, yet they're ready to quit their job, sign a lease, hire employees, print business cards, open shop, and wait for the hordes of customers.

Here's a perfect example of "bad plan, bad model." Against my advice, a client bought a diner. He was the proverbial intellectual—right down to the Ph.D.—who was sick of his desk job. As smart as he was, he had problems right from the start. The seller misled him about the profitability of the business. That was easy to understand because the restaurant was a local institution with a long, storied history. Then he discovered that he couldn't raise his prices—even though the cost of everything else was skyrocketing. The customers balked at paying any more than they had years ago when their parents took them there for breakfast. Give the guy credit. He worked hard and hoped for the best. He thought he could succeed, if he just tried harder. So he worked fourteen hours a day, until everyone told him he looked like a walking heart attack. He stopped taking a paycheck. He also got his girlfriend to wait tables and work the cash register, also without pay. Meanwhile, his employees—the ones he could get—threatened to quit unless they got raises and the customers threatened never to come back unless he lowered the prices. Not exactly a model for profitability.

The whole situation could have been avoided had he simply asked himself, "If we have this many customers, and we charge this much per meal, and it costs this much to run the place, will we have a profit or a loss?" Yet in his mind, developing a business plan was way too complex, like predicting the weather or reading instruction manuals.

Nine months after taking ownership and probably hours shy of his first heart attack, he closed the diner and walked away licking his wounds. This was a business that couldn't produce a profit, much less attract a buyer.

## Developing a Successful Business Plan

So what should you do? Simple. Develop a plan. Here's how you do that:

- Create a list of every major thing you need to operate your business.

- List all of the key employees you will need.

- Survey the market for prices of similar products and services and then set your prices with a clear reason why your prices should be any different from your competitors' prices.

- Project the revenues, expenses, and cash flow for your business for the first three years of operation.

- In evaluating your competition, describe what advantages your competition has over you and what advantages you have over your competition, including your competitors' likely response to your business and your plan for maintaining advantages over your competitors.

- Describe your competition in detail, what products/services they sell and at what prices and how they will affect your ability to sell your products and services at your predicted prices.

- Explain your sources of capital to start and continue your business, as well as contingency plans for cash reserves, lines of credit, and/or raising additional funds.

- List the various potential locations for your business and the pros and cons of each location, including different costs and revenues associated with each location.

- Research and describe what business or investor might want to buy or invest in your business and why. Include how you will shape your business to appeal to these parties.

- Determine the best legal structure for your business. Include a description of how this structure will help you raise start-up capital, borrow money, and govern, grow, and, ultimately, sell your business.

- Describe where the market for your product is headed, what forces are driving this market, and what strategy you will employ to address these forces and the changing market.

I know what you're thinking. Admit it. You're eager to get started. You just want to forget the whole complicated "plan" thing and plunge in. Before you jump—off that cliff—remember the time you tried to build a model or assemble a bicycle or cook a complicated meal and you decided not to read the instructions. Remember how you worked so hard and ended up with a mess. Remember, most businesses fail. Now get back to putting together a good business plan.

Then take your plan to your lawyer, your accountant, a banker, and a mentor if you have one. Ask for their opinions. Tell them to be blunt. Better now than when it's too late, when you've folded shop and have to ask for your old job back. No one wants to see that.

Also, regularly review and update your plan. You need to stick with your plan and avoid distractions. But you also need to revise your plan to take into account new and changing factors.

Oh, and read the rest of the book or you're bound to screw up somewhere else.

Back to my old buddy Alex. He kept piling up the profits. He had a good plan and a profitable business model. Success bred believers. When the checks kept coming in, our old gang finally admitted that Alex took the right path. And some executives of a large advertising company saw Alex's billboards sprouting up and customers peeling away to advertise with him. They dug deeper. They saw the long-term leases that provided great billboard locations for modest rental fees. They saw the constant demand for advertising. They saw profits that grew year after year. So they bought Alex's business for a small fortune.

Not that it changed him. Alex still doesn't shave regularly. He drives a beat-up old car and lives in a modest house. But Alex is content and quite wealthy as he continues down that road less traveled.

# 3

## Your Competitive Edge

### *What Makes You So Special?*

It was early in the bagel craze, long before the phrases "low-carb" and "South Beach" were part of the vocabulary. My client Carl had half a dozen franchises in the D.C. area. He was making serious money and life was a party.

"Carl, you need to sell your stores," said me, the party pooper.

"Are you crazy?" he asked. "Every store I open is a moneymaker. I'm bringing in almost a million dollars a year. Pretty impressive for a guy with a high school education." Carl had, in fact, built a successful chain of stores, but only because he got in early. The head start and some advertising helped, but in business that's never enough. He didn't realize he had a target on his back. "Sure, I'm getting a lot of big-buck offers to sell," he bragged. "But why in the world would I?"

"Because you have no competitive edge," I explained, introducing a term every businessperson desperately needs to know. "That million dollars a year you're bringing in is going to be noticed by the competition. Well-funded competition. Overwhelming competition. What are you going to do when they start selling bagels for less? Are you going to be able to offer something different so you stand apart? Like what? Bagels without holes? I've seen it before in other feast-or-famine businesses. Do the words 'frozen yogurt' mean anything to you? Listen to me. Sell while the selling is good."

"No way," he answered, with words he would soon eat.

## Competitive Edge: A Definition

You might have a profitable business model, but without a competitive edge you can't fend off the copycats. Henry Ford didn't invent the automobile. Instead, he created the assembly line to produce cars faster and cheaper. That was his competitive edge. The guy who invented the automobile—well, we don't even remember his name, much less know what happened to him.

Care and compassion for your clients can also give you a competitive edge. When was the last time your doctor called you after an appointment to see how you were doing? And if he or she did call, would you tell other people and use that doctor as long as you could? Of course you would. Each business presents different opportunities to distinguish its goods and services.

In other businesses, a competitive edge can be a something less tangible to your customers but very profitable for you. For instance, you can get a competitive edge from a contract that gives your company an advantage, such as exclusive rights to a key ingredient, or a "most favored nation" clause that guarantees you better pricing. Your competitive edge might come from a patent or trade secret or extensive training of employees.

One of my clients, Joe, has a great small business. Part of his success lies in his ability to keep a low profile, so we'll fudge a bit from his actual business and say he sells towels to pro sports teams. Joe knows the coaches and the players, so he's ahead of the game in that respect. Even more so, he provides incredible service. Most days he can be found in his little cubbyhole of an office, on the phone attending to every detail. Some players like bigger towels; others, only designer brands. Some franchises want towels in their team colors; others just want the least expensive. Joe's attention to service was enough to get him going in the business but not enough to keep him there forever. So one day I told him he was vulnerable to any competitor who wanted to go after him by cutting prices or developing their own friendships with coaches and trainers. Fortunately, Joe listened, which was how I helped him implement a powerful competitive edge.

We pursued it from all sides. To lock up the towel wholesalers, we convinced them that the volume and prestige of our business justified giving us better prices and terms. Then we were able to go to the teams and guarantee them the best deal. In fact, if anyone could beat us, we'd refund the difference. In exchange, the teams signed long-term exclusive contracts with us. The benefits kept multiplying. With the better terms, we signed up more teams. Because of his great service, ironclad contracts, and guaranteed low prices, Joe has established an overwhelming competitive edge. Regardless of your business, to succeed in the long run, you need the same thing—a competitive edge.

Which is something Carl the bagel seller learned the hard way. He didn't like my advice to sell and dropped out of contact for a while. But then one day he called with the news.

"Jack, you were wrong," he said.

"Oh?" I wondered.

"Yes," Carl revealed. "You told me that I was at the top and should sell. Well, I didn't actually hit 'the top' of the market until six months after we talked. You were right about everything else. The competition came in, snagged a big piece of the market by undercutting my prices, and wiped out my profits. At first I limped along. The stores that made money kept the losers afloat. But eventually, we had to put most of the stores into bankruptcy."

Carl continued, "Fortunately, I saved *some* of my profits. But if I had sold when you told me to, I'd be calling from my Cessna right now. Painful lesson learned."

In the end, Carl had to close each store or sell them for bargain-basement prices. He had experienced one of the most painful and critical lessons of building a business. Successful businesses can't just be profitable at the outset. To remain successful over the long haul, and eventually sell your business, you need a *competitive edge*.

# 4

## Scalability

### *Because Size Does Matter*

People who put their nose to the grindstone get a lot of bloody noses.

Typical entrepreneurs endure long hours and rarely take vacations. They toil at their desks most weekends, while slowly becoming strangers to their family and friends. Yet for all that hard work, many never realize the tremendous potential of their business. They never grow it to the next level or sell it for a lot of money. It's a shame, but they just don't know any better. Instead, they retire frustrated and bitter or even broken. Someone simply told them, "Work hard and you'll do fine." If it were only that simple.

You do need to work hard to be successful. But you also need more. One of the most important is scalability.

Scalability is, simply, the ability to grow your business. Scalability is not how big you are. Scalability is how big you can get.

Why is scalability important? So you can sell your business for a lot of money. Remember, people buy businesses to make money. Purchasers won't buy a company for $100 million if it's never going to be worth more than that. Where's the profit on their investment? Instead, they need to be able to expand the business and make it worth more. It is not unusual for buyers to expect to double their money in five years—and that, my friend, comes from growing the business. When buyers are considering your business, it is critical that they see this scalability. If your business is built for growth, they're going to jump at the chance to buy your business. You can sell, reap the benefits, and relax.

So, how do you get scalable? Well, scalability means different things for different businesses. These are various examples of the attributes that create the ability to grow:

**SUPPLY OF GOODS:** You just opened an art gallery. You have a bunch of artists but only one who's really selling. As soon as you put one of his paintings on the wall, it sells—regardless of price. But this artist takes three months to finish each painting. Without other popular art, you're not scalable.

**RECRUITING:** You're that rare accounting firm that "gets" your clients. You provide excellent service in a surprisingly understandable manner. Even your fees are reasonable. Face it: Your clients love you. Maybe too much. Now you're overwhelmed. You're not returning calls quickly, you're taking too long to turn around the work, and you're postponing meetings, all because you don't have enough help. Without a program to hire and train new employees to meet growing demand, you're not scalable.

**BANKING AND BORROWING:** Truck owners love the new reinforced aluminum doublewheels you sell. To meet demand, you need to place bigger orders with the manufacturer of the wheels, and that requires ever larger cash deposits. You're proud of the fact that you never borrowed a penny—and it worked for your small business. But now you can't pay for everything out of your pocket. To meet customer demand, you need a banking relationship that will enable you to borrow money. Without this ability to borrow, you don't have scalability.

**INFRASTRUCTURE:** Business is booming at your thriving little organic grocery store. This would be great news, except you never planned on being such a success. You were too worried about making it past day one. Your building, computers, and phones can't handle the volume. You're also locked into a long-term lease for a store that's way too small. In fact, your customers' greatest frustration is crowded parking, long lines, and empty bins because you can't restock fast enough in such a small space. You thought small. Without planning for growth, you're not scalable.

Let me highlight this for you: **scalability is a mind-set**. It's about constantly making decisions that create bridges, not barriers, to growth.

## Thinking About Tomorrow

Too many business decisions fail to consider scalability. Consider this scenario: you're about to hire a bookkeeper. Sure, a bookkeeper is critical for getting the bills paid, making deposits, and keeping simple books straight. Most new businesses and even well-established small businesses get by with these basics. But do you just want to "get by"? You need to think scalable if you want to grow.

Try the scalable approach. Hire a Chief Financial Officer with an MBA. Now you have someone looking at your key indicators and figuring out when your business will pick up or slow down and how to adjust accordingly. Your CFO is crunching the numbers, showing you where you're making money and should expand and where you're losing cash and should cut back. Your CFO is successfully handling your banking and investor relationships. High fives all around.

I know what you're thinking: a CFO is going to cost you more money. Or not. The reality is, your CFO will more than pay for him- or herself in the long run. Here's how. Hire a recent graduate. Get someone who has great skills but not a lot of experience. He or she will take a lower salary in exchange for the opportunity to grow with your business. Remember, the CFO is going to help you make better financial decisions, so your company is going to make more money and waste less. Think of the extra cash you'll have just by paying less for your borrowing and earning more on your deposits. Better still, your CFO will take a lot of weight off your shoulders, so you're freed up to run the company.

The problem is, most of you still aren't going to do it. On the surface, you say scalability makes sense. But then you tell yourself it costs too much. Or you're too busy to deal with it. Or you're not ready for it yet. Or . . . *stop*. I've heard all the excuses.

We need to talk.

The biggest scalability challenge of all is you.

## Founder's Dilemma: A One-Person Show

Let me tell you about "Derek," and see if any of this sounds familiar. Derek started his company ten years ago in a sublet office no bigger than a bathroom. Now he has a few dozen employees and $10 million a year in sales. Despite the growth, Derek still personally performs every major job. He lands all of his company's major contracts—which, by the way, should go to his far larger and more established competitors. Much to his customers' delight, he can be reached 24/7/365 and calls every customer every week. His clients swear by him and marvel at his energy and accessibility. Derek does it all.

Sounds good, doesn't it? It's not. It's a problem. It's a big problem called the Founder's Dilemma.

The Founder's Dilemma is like a Shakespearean flaw: what makes you strong also makes you weak. The things that drove his company's initial success—his micromanagement, his perfectionism, and more— now limit his company's further growth. That's the crazy thing. The very attributes that help a start-up business become a successful small business undermine the ability to grow further.

Let me explain. Derek started his business with a lot to prove. Maybe he wasn't a good athlete and people made fun of him, or maybe he was a good athlete and he blew out his knee and everyone thought, "Derek's done." Maybe some girlfriend left him. Maybe his parents didn't love him. Maybe he felt poor or stupid or ugly. You wouldn't believe how many successful entrepreneurs burn the midnight oil because of a bad self-image. Everyone's story is different. But they all have something to prove. They want to prove that they are good, that they are not a failure or a loser. And do they ever work to prove it.

Derek got into the office early. He stayed late. He worked despite fever and chills, birthdays and anniversaries. On the rare occasions he went to dinner with the family or made it to his son's soccer game, Derek was still taking business calls with the Bluetooth headset that became part of his anatomy. He pounded after opportunities that scared off others, talking his way through doors that were shut for countless competitors. The victories came. He landed some big accounts. He became profitable. He hired a crowd of assistants. He won business awards and accolades. Derek became a success. And Derek was hooked.

He didn't have his parents' love, that old girlfriend didn't come back, and he didn't have the cheers of the stadium crowd. But he had a substitute that felt pretty good: business success. So Derek became his business and his business became his identity.

But now Derek can't let go. He can't delegate. He can't groom others to take over his many roles. He can't support them in their training and growth. He can't let them make mistakes and learn to become better leaders. His personal attention to detail is a bottleneck. Every day, there's a line of employees outside his office, all waiting for approval of minutiae before they can proceed with their projects. Instead of building a management team to run the company, Derek is in the weeds deciding the weight of the paper for the company's new stationery.

## Inside Derek's Head

Derek had tried once to build an executive team and delegate. He hired a top-notch VP of sales to build and manage a sales team. But then, as would be expected and encouraged, the VP did something special. He landed a big new piece of new business. Everyone gathered in the conference room to listen to the VP's war story. They smiled approvingly and applauded his success.

That's when a little voice inside Derek said, "If he can do that, then I'm not really so special, after all. If this keeps up, my company won't even need me." Derek was threatened by the VP. In fact, the better the VP did, the more Derek was threatened. So he made the VP's life a living hell. Derek gave him menial tasks, berated him in front of other employees, canceled his vacations, and set him up for failure with a grueling schedule and impossible expectations.

Derek had to be the star. If Derek was on a basketball team, he wouldn't pass a lot, especially around the basket.

Here's why it matters to you: because all entrepreneurs have some Derek in them and it's hurting their companies. They can change. You can change.

## Overcoming the Founder's Dilemma

To overcome the Founder's Dilemma, first redefine success. Instead of your achievements, success should mean the accomplishments of others.

Second, change from being star of the team to coach—from being Michael Jordan to Phil Jackson. In Derek's case, bragging, "Hey, I brought in another contract," must change to praising, "Hey, my VP of sales brought in another contract." Your job is now to support the accomplishments of others and of the entire company.

Third, get good people. Hire the best people you can afford. When you delegate, you'll get better results. Without these good results, you'll likely revert to trying to do it all yourself.

Fourth, get some counseling. Change is hard. And this is all about change. I know what you're thinking here: "I'm not crazy." Putting that debate aside for a moment, understand that we all have issues. If you bear any of the characteristics of Derek, your identity is too married to your business and your self-esteem is going to crater without it. After all, what are you living for, a solid gold coffin? Effective counseling will help you enjoy the game without scoring every point.

Fifth, reconnect with family and friends. Get a hobby. Develop other ways of enjoying life.

Sixth, and finally, remember the goal. A purchaser is not buying *you*. Build a *company* that's attractive to a purchaser.

# 5

# Bench Strength

## *Your Executive Team*

In high school, when *The Lord of the Rings* was just a book series, Tommy was the guy drawing pictures of warriors with enormous biceps who slammed swords down on the heads of fire-breathing dragons. Now Tommy is the founder of Whack-Job, LLC, a small software company that makes video games that run on PlayStation, Wii, and Xbox. He comes up with the ideas and his staff, mostly high school buddies, program. The reviewers loved his first game, *Zombie Wedding: Cauldron of Death*, although sales were disappointing because of manufacturing glitches and a lousy distributor. Despite that, fans are clamoring on the blogs for *Cauldron II*. But Tommy's realizing that he's wearing too many hats and needs help. Aside from inventing the games, Tommy gets lunch for the gang, fixes the paper jams in the photocopier, answers the phones, calls in the payroll, and pays the bills.

Tommy is not really running a company. He's running errands. He needs to build an executive team—or his dream of building and selling his business is going to end up in its very own cauldron of death.

### Bench Strength: Building Your Team

With the advice of a good consultant, Tommy begins building his bench strength. "Bench strength" means having a team of executives that can run each of your critical business operations. Unlike the "bench" on a sports team, these are no second-stringers. These are your stars.

At Whack-Job, Tommy's first executive hire is a Chief Operating Officer. The new COO has experience running a company day to day. She is also capable of handling a variety of tasks, from moving the business out of Tommy's basement and into a warehouse, to searching for a new manufacturer and distributor, to helping recruit additional executives. With Tommy freed up and the COO tackling the company's weaknesses, *Cauldron II* should please more than the critics and achieve financial success.

It works. *Cauldron II* is a smash hit. No self-respecting fifteen-year-old alienated, semi-Goth gamer is without it. Woo-hoo!

To stay on the cutting edge, Tommy and the COO quickly realize, Whack-Job also needs a Chief Technology Officer. Sure, the programmers know a lot. But the company should have an expert to find technological advancements, speed production, improve efficiency, and enhance the finished product for the customer. So they recruit a CTO away from a leading video-game producer. The new CTO immediately replaces outdated equipment and systems, improves game graphics and special features, and speeds *Cauldron III* to market while the franchise is still hot. Cha-ching!

Now Whack-Job has money in the bank. They're ready to ramp up hiring and diversify their video-game product line. It's time for a Director of Human Resources to hire and manage the growing workforce. The company also needs a Chief Financial Officer to manage company finances, build a banking relationship, and start cultivating ties in the investment-banking world that could lead to a future sale of the company. With just a few executives, you can begin to transform your company.

## Executive Recruiting

Whether it's Whack-Job or your company, the right executives are essential to the growth of a business. So where do you start? First, decide which position will add the most value to your business. What type of executive will free up the founders to do their jobs while adding experience and expertise the founders don't have? Identifying the players you need is the first step in building bench strength.

Second, determine how you're going to recruit. Too many people make a big mistake by only considering people they know. Cast a broader net. Your needs may be better filled by advertising or hiring a recruiter. Be aware that advertising can attract people who are out of a job—sometimes with good reason—or at least unhappy where they are working. A recruiter may be able to find top talent who aren't necessarily looking and might be tempted by an attractive job offer.

There are two types of recruiters. Retained agencies are paid a fixed fee to conduct an extensive search, interview job candidates, conduct background checks, and even assist in interviewing and negotiating. These agencies are paid whether or not you hire one of their selections, although most retained agencies will search until they're successful. Retained agencies often are hired by the same company for multiple searches over the course of a long-term relationship. These agencies are more expensive but also more focused on finding a good match and keeping you happy.

Contingency recruiters are paid only when their candidates are hired by an employer. These recruiters receive a fee equal to a percentage of your new employee's initial annual salary. While the starting point can be as high as 33 percent of first-year compensation, these fees are negotiable. The norm, especially for repeat customers, is 15 to 25 percent.

Usually contingency agencies offer a limited guarantee, such as a replacement recruit if the first hire does not stay with you for three to six months. Less often, the agency will provide a partial refund. The benefit of a contingent search is obvious. You don't pay if you don't hire. However, because these agencies are only paid when you hire, some shortcut their due diligence and overlook bad matches.

Whether you are working with a retained or contingent agency, pick a specialist. Many recruiters find only a particular type of employee, such as nurses, software programmers, or CFOs.

Make sure that you are a big fish in your recruiter's pond. To get the best candidates, you need to be a priority for your recruiter. Likewise, watch out for recruiters who funnel their best candidates to a favored client (who ain't you!).

Third, do your own due diligence. Once you've selected a few candidates, you and your colleagues should interview each candidate several times. Many candidates ace their first meeting, then fall apart during a second or third interview. These crumbling candidates don't feel worthy of the job and sabotage themselves as it gets closer to reality. Multiple interviews help weed out candidates who make a good first impression but aren't up to the challenge. You should also compare the answers that a candidate gives to different people. Consistency, or the lack of it, is a great way to judge honesty.

Due diligence also means background checks. You don't want to be the "genius" who hires the CFO who embezzled from his last job. In today's world, effective due diligence requires smarts and creativity. Google searches, even MySpace and Facebook pages, can reveal conduct or character that will nix a job offer. In other cases, bogus credentials can be discovered by getting college transcripts sent directly to you from the school. You may need to hire a security company to check court, criminal, credit, and other records. Ask for references and try to talk to past employers. Understand that most former employers won't give an honest reference anymore. They are too afraid of being sued for slander to tell you what they really think. But some will talk, and you never know what you'll learn.

Bottom line: your bench strength is vital to your success. Don't hire some smooth talker in a nice suit who proves to be all style and no substance.

*Note of caution: consult an attorney and make sure your due diligence and hiring processes are legal.*

## Mirror, Mirror on the Wall

Let's face it. You need to overcome your own issues to build an executive team. It is not unusual to feel threatened when you relinquish power and the limelight. Every dollar you pay may feel like it is coming right out of your own personal Ferrari fund. You may balk at hiring a truly gifted executive.

When I suggest building bench strength, I'm often met with skepticism: "Why do I need an executive team?" Because:

1. You're not going to grow without it.

2. Bench strength makes your company attractive to potential buyers.

3. Without it, you could die. Not go into bankruptcy but die—as in casket, funeral, people weeping, and flowers. Overwork and stress do that.

Next question: "How much is this going to cost me?" Simple:

1. Much more than you want to spend.

2. Much less than it will cost you if you don't do it.

Business owners often say they can't afford to bring on expensive employees. If that's true, wait until you can. More often, owners really mean they don't want to spend their money on people. They don't see the value. I've heard the "affordability" reason from an owner who spends six figures every year entertaining at luxury football and baseball skyboxes. That's hardly a case where the company can't afford it. It's a question of how you want to spend your money. So let's all recognize that money is an issue and deal with it.

## The Pay Issue

When you're attracting executives, you have to be prepared for new demands. Good executives aren't cheap and they aren't sheep.

Take executive salaries. A common rookie mistake is being too cost conscious. Owners will reject their top candidate because she costs more than another. Too often, owners focus on the hit to the bottom line or how they never made that kind of salary when they started. That's short-term thinking. The value of a successful hire is immense and lasting. The difference between a good executive and a bad one can be millions of dollars, can be the success or failure of countless ventures and maybe even your company.

You may also have to bend your own rules or create new ones. For instance, you may not offer disability income insurance or stock options and bonus programs. But any and all of those could be necessary to attract the executive you're recruiting. To get an executive to leave her current job, you may even have to promise a large severance package if you fire her. So brace yourself, because you're going to have to accept some things you're not used to.

Many of the best and brightest know what they're worth, and they're going to insist on that—and often more. I always tell my clients to research the market and be prepared to top it. You almost can't overpay. "Huh?" is the usual response. "Can't overpay! You gotta be kidding me."

Here's how it works. Say you want to pay a $200,000 salary for your first executive and the best candidate wants $300,000. You have no question that he really is the best candidate. You just think he wants too much money. Hire him. Pay the $300K. And comfort yourself with the following: put your new executive on a secret six-month probation. Don't tell him. No one needs that kind of pressure. If he's not worth the $300K, you should know by the end of six months and you will only be out the extra $50K you spent in that time period. But if he really is The One and he earns his keep, you're on the way to one of your most profitable decisions ever. So, you've got $50K on the one hand and great riches on the other. Seems like a fair trade-off.

A few pointers to remember about the pay issue:

- A person is more motivated if he believes he is paid what he's worth. Conversely the person who feels shortchanged will—consciously or not—hold back and not give the new job their all.

- While the company owners and key personnel should have input, negotiating the employment terms should be delegated to your outside recruiter and employment lawyer. You don't want any friction from negotiations carrying over into working relationships once the person is hired.

- Most of all, don't let the negotiations become contentious. You don't want someone who's battle scarred and bitter working for you. You want a win-win, where both the employer and the employee are happy with the result. If you can't achieve that, politely end the negotiations. You both need to move on.

Be forewarned, you can also become bitter. I've seen owners go through the hiring process, take time to select just the right person, negotiate a lucrative pay package—and then barely give their new hire a folding chair, a beat-up desk, and a pencil to do his job. The owner is clearly upset about spending so much money and now is sabotaging the new employee's efforts. Instead of giving the new executive the tools to succeed, the owner slashes the executive's budget, doesn't allow him to build his own team, and forces him to do more with less. You need to let your executive team do their jobs the right way.

It is also critical to establish and communicate the role of each new executive. Clearly define her duties, as well as her place in the chain of command—to whom she reports and who reports to her. Determine and communicate this role *before* you hire her, and then communicate it again to everyone with whom she works.

It is unfortunate, but you also need to be prepared to lose some of those people who can't accept these changes. Hiring executives, especially the first few times, has a tendency to ruffle feathers. Some employees will feel hurt and rejected because they lose special access to the owners or because they realize that they were not considered executive material. You can cushion the blow by keeping them informed of the process and letting them vent. If it is realistic, you can also show them that there is a path for their own growth within the company. No matter what you do, some may quit and you should be prepared for that reality.

It will take time for you to assemble your executive team. It will take even longer for their leadership and decisions to bear fruit. Successfully investing in bench strength requires skill, patience, and money. It may also help to know that this path is well worn by many small-business owners who tackled the same hurdles. They discovered, as will you, that a good executive team pays for itself many times over.

# 6

## Sustainability

### *Surviving Until You Succeed*

Fritz was finally going to show everyone, all the doubters. He was finally going to make it rich in the real estate business. He finally had his dream project.

He started off great. A local government had agreed to sell him land for an unbelievably low price, well below market value. The land was perfect, ideally located right next to a brand-new highway and large enough for several spacious buildings. With a number of months before he needed to close on the deal, Fritz thought big. He began planning to build retail and office space that would rent for millions of dollars per year. He hired the best architects and engineers to design stunning stores, underground parking, and gleaming office buildings that would stand like monuments at a bend in the highway. He ordered all of the required—and expensive—surveys, studies, and tests. He put graphic artists on the payroll to prepare slick brochures and Web sites to help him market the project. He started negotiating with large businesses to lease key portions of the project.

Then Fritz ran out of money.

The whole project imploded. Fritz stopped the architects and engineers and lawyers and graphic artists. Fritz dropped the lease negotiations. Fritz didn't return a lot of calls. All he ever said to his secretary was, "Take a message." Until he fired her.

Everything stopped, except the vultures. A local heavyweight swooped in and "offered" to take over the project and let Fritz keep a small percentage. Fritz really had no choice. He could have either little or nothing.

What went wrong? It's simple. Fritz didn't start out with enough money. He began with a few hundred thousand dollars when he needed a few million. That's right, a few million dollars. He wasn't building a house; he was building a small city. How else was he going to pay for the plans and studies? How else was he going to pay a staff? How else was he going to hire the attorneys to negotiate all of the leases? How else was he going to see the project through to the end?

Maybe Fritz didn't see that he needed a lot more money—or maybe he didn't want to see. He never admitted it to me, but I suspect that after years as a real estate broker he was tired of helping other people get rich. He had found plenty of others their own land and tenants, lenders and architects. He had negotiated their deals and advised them on how to get it done. Heck, except for sticking a shovel in the ground, he had done it all—for others. So he was impatient to succeed in a big way, maybe so impatient that it blinded him.

Like so many hopeful entrepreneurs, Fritz paid a steep price for starting a business without enough money. Sure, he put on a brave face and acted as if bringing in another developer was just a hiccup (you know, like General Custer's last "hiccup" at Little Bighorn). But no one goes from 100 percent of a big deal to a tiny percentage without learning a big life lesson: start with enough money to see your business through to consistent profitability.

It business terms, this is sustainability. It is the ability to sustain, or stay in, business despite economic cycles and unexpected difficulties. Let me explain:

Sustainability means starting with enough capital to get you to the point where you are consistently profitable. It means adopting practices unique to your business to get through tough times, like setting aside reserves or creating disaster recovery plans or buying special insurance. Finally, sustainability means persistence, not blind refusal to accept reality but an enduring faith in your business and the mental fortitude to drive on despite difficulty.

For so many entrepreneurs like Fritz a lack of capital is the biggest reason new businesses fail. Let's say that again: lack of capital is the biggest reason new businesses fail. Now, let's say it out loud. Tell your friends and family. Write a haiku.

Lack of capital
is the biggest reason
new businesses fail.

There are large craters—figuratively—throughout the business world dug by countless undercapitalized businesses that crashed to earth, plowed into the ground, and burst into flames. Whether it's inexperience or impatience, denial or hope, too many entrepreneurs start without enough cash. In their minds, their business plan seems solid. Fritz thought a great buy on a piece of land could carry his business, but he didn't make sure he had enough cash to survive.

I've seen the mistake made in virtually every type of business:

- A furniture store didn't have enough money to pay manufacturers to ship products. Customers tired of waiting for their living-room sets, so they demanded refunds and went elsewhere.

- A techie start-up gambled and saved a few grand by not registering their trademarks. A big competitor—who had paid for trademarks—entered the market with a similar name and began drawing away customers.

- A dance studio lost their best instructors—and clients with them—because the studio couldn't afford to pay enough and provide benefits.

Too many entrepreneurs tell themselves, "I have enough money to open the doors. I'll figure out the rest later." But problems don't go away just because you ignore them. I learned that the hard way when I was five. I was playing with matches and started a fire in the woods behind my house. After a few futile attempts at putting it out, I walked away and hoped for the best. That actually worked, for about a half hour. But my small fire turned into a three-fire-truck blaze and burned down the entire woods. At a tender age, I saw that you need to confront your problems. Starting a business without enough money and hoping for the best is like walking away from a small fire.

So, the question budding entrepreneurs should be asking them-selves from the start is . . .

## How Much Start-up Cash Is Enough?

The secret to determining how much start-up capital you need is "do-ing the math." Get out your business plan and follow these five easy steps to calculate the minimum amount of cash you need to launch your business:

1. Estimate how long it will take from start-up until you are profitable on a regular basis. No one has a crystal ball, but typically you are looking at six to eighteen months, longer for more complicated businesses. For simplicity's sake, let's call this time the launch period.

2. Calculate all of your expenses for the launch period. For example, let's say these expenses are $1 million.

3. Estimate your revenues for the launch period. Again, let's say these revenues are $300,000. By definition, when you are in the launch period, you are not profitable, so it is inevitable that your expenses are going to be more than your revenues.

4. Now calculate the total of your expenses minus the total of your revenues for the launch period. In our example, the

$1,000,000 of expenses minus the $300,000 in revenues leaves us with an initial deficit of $700,000. This initial deficit isn't how much cash you need to start your business, but we are getting closer to determining your initial capital requirement.

5. Add money for potential problems. I recommend adding anywhere from 10 to 30 percent of the initial deficit.

- Use the lower end of this range if you are more certain about your estimates and there are less likely to be surprises in your business.

- Add more money if you were doing more guessing than estimating. Also, add cash if your business is riskier or if you are going to be spending a lot early on before you have any significant revenues.

So, in our example, because the initial deficit is $700,000, you would add anywhere from $70,000 to $210,000. This means your initial capital requirement is $770,000 to $910,000. While this is just an example, in many cases your initial capital requirement is a big bundle of cash that you need in the bank, ready to go. You're going to face a lot of challenges. Don't let running out of money be one of them.

Most people don't start with the right amount of money. If you calculated how much you need and you don't have enough, here are a few key pointers:

- Banks are not big on lending to start-ups. If you have a track record of establishing successful businesses, you have a much better chance. If not, look elsewhere.

- Potential investors tend to evaporate (you'll have more luck with a painting "party").

- When people do invest, they invest in success. You need enough money to make it look like you don't need theirs. Don't plan on raising a ton of money with business cards printed at Kinko's and "business meetings" at Starbucks. Have enough cash for securities lawyers to draw up the prospectus and other investment documents, to take pretty pictures and make brochures, et cetera. You need money to raise money.

- Borrow from family and friends with great reluctance, like you're asking them to donate an organ. The downside of losing Dad's retirement money should be evident.

- Save.

- If you don't have enough money, wait or scale back. Warning: Scaling back is tricky; you may cut meat instead of fat. So waiting may be better.

## Savvy Substitutes

It is possible to start small and without much cash, to build a business from scratch and to make it sustainable. One of my clients did it perfectly. His plan was to sell vitamins and supplements. He started by buying a mailing list from a similar company that was going out of business. Customers slowly started ordering his products through the mail. When he had saved enough money, he rented a warehouse that was so out of the way, I could have given you perfect directions and you still wouldn't find it. But the location became part of its charm. You were considered hip if you could find it, like some LA hole-in-the-wall bar.

My client worked hard, didn't waste a penny, and even brought in his mom to help—for free. He built up a great selection and specialized in natural supplements. Prices were low, the staff was knowledgeable, and he would special-order anything you wanted. Eventually, he came up with catchy advertising that brought in crowds. Working slowly and modestly, he expanded, but always by renting cheap space in edgy neighborhoods that other retailers overlooked. Then he would draw the customers there with his service, selection, and pricing. It took years, but now he has a chain of stores and his business remains strong. Starting cheap and small can work.

It's rare, but you can also find substitutes for start-up capital.

In addition to starting cheap and small, I've found another miracle substitute for initial capital: contracts and customers. If you have several customers who've signed on the dotted line guaranteeing you income for an extended period of time, you can successfully launch a business without much money. Zach proves the point. He was a CPA who did financial analysis for a private hedge fund. When he left to start his own financial-consulting firm, the hedge fund became his first client, putting Zach on a twelve-month retainer, equal to his old salary. The retainer paid his rent and his assistant's salary and covered the rest of Zach's monthly overhead. He ultimately added a lot of clients and a team of other consultants, but that first contract ended the need for a big chunk of start-up capital.

## In the Long Run

In the long run, sustainability is also about establishing practices for surviving downtimes and disasters. Depending on your business, these practices can range from establishing reserves (think about the banks and brokers that got sucked into the subprime black hole), to creating a disaster recovery plan (think Katrina and New Orleans businesses), to buying insurance (think about any fire on the eleven o'clock news).

Early in my career I saw a particularly harsh example of how the failure to protect against a downturn could crush a business and the guy who ran it. Lance was breaking into the real estate development business in the heady mid-1980s. Times were so good and sloppy that banks would let you borrow if you could sign your name. You could put 10 percent down on a large commercial project and borrow the rest. Lance built an office complex and then a shopping center and then another and another and another and another, each time borrowing the maximum 90 percent of his costs. He could have borrowed less, but the gold rush was on and he was eager to grow. All of this worked quite well, for a while. Lance grew rich and moved the family into a big mansion with a full-size indoor basketball court. His wood-paneled office looked like something out of an English castle. He got a warehouse for his car collection. You get the picture. Then recession hit in the late eighties. Retailers such as drugstores and department stores started filing for bankruptcy and stopped paying Lance the rent. He still had giant mortgages but now only a dwindling stream of cash coming in. Worse yet, Lance had personally guaranteed everything. He couldn't make the payments due on his real estate empire. The budget was just too tight. His business started going down the tubes. The banks foreclosed and Lance lost all of his shopping centers and his cars, his cash, and finally his house. He and his family were forced to move into a rental.

Later Lance reflected on his rags-to-riches-to-rags journey. He realized that, at the very least, he should have taken some chips off the table, sold a couple of his shopping centers, paid down his debt, and created a reserve for bad times.

Also, consider the following:

**DO YOUR HOMEWORK:** Countless losses can be avoided by kicking the tires hard. If you want to launch a new product or enter a new market or hire a new executive or buy another business, do your due diligence.

**DIVERSIFY:** Your business shouldn't depend on one or just a few customers or products. At the beginning, diversification should not be a major concern. However, as the business becomes established try to avoid having any single customers exceed 10 to 20 percent of your sales.

**LIMIT YOUR LIABILITY:** Early on, you and your business may have to guarantee everything, from loans, to leases, to every other contract you sign. But as your track record and leverage increase, negotiate limits on your exposure.

**BE ANALYTICAL, NOT WISHFUL:** With every venture, plan for break-even, profitable, and money-losing results.

Lance's experience seared into me an ages-old lesson, one that I have taught my clients ever since: trees don't grow to the sky. Have a cash cushion. Plan for bad times. Build sustainability into your business.

# 7

## Personal Sustainability

*Playing Until You Win*

Building and selling a business is rarely a sprint. Think marathon instead.

Just like you need a sustainable business, you need personal sustainability, too. You can't run a company from a hospital bed. You need to show up. You're not going to overcome the many challenges you'll undoubtedly face unless you're able to work hard. How do you do that? The answer is the same thing you've been hearing since you were a kid: proper diet, exercise, and sleep.

Don't get me wrong. I know many successful businesspeople who get their only exercise unwrapping candy bars. So I can't say that you have to healthy to be successful. But if you're looking for an edge, here it is.

That edge propels entrepreneurs through sixty-hour workweeks. It keeps their energy up when they need it. I've seen people scoring points in a late-night negotiation because they were still sharp and the opposition could hardly keep their eyes open and focus.

A dear friend of mine built a $100 million business. While he was on the way there, the nightly nachos and cheese snacks had started to show. So he began working out. He soon realized the more he exercised, the more energy he had. He became more productive at work. He saw that a healthy diet also reduced his downtime from sickness. Call me crazy, but that hour-long workout actually saved him time. It improved not just his health but also his performance at work and ultimately the success of his company.

Look at great athletes. Cal Ripken, Joe Montana, and Michael Jordan had tremendous talent, but they achieved historic victories because they were healthy enough to stay in the game. As the quote goes, "Half of winning is showing up."

## Persistence

This one is not optional.

With any luck, you will be in business long enough to have some bad luck. Recession strikes and customers stop buying your houses. A competitor steals your best software programmers with promises of stock options that you can't match. Medicare policy changes and the government reimbursements for your CT scans plunge.

Whatever the reason, there are going to be dark days when you will be tempted to pull the sheets over your head, stay in bed, and give up. Don't.

The solution is persistence.

Persistence is the mental fortitude that drives you to kick the sheets off the bed, put your feet on the floor, and march forward. Despite the repeated threat of failure, countless entrepreneurs have persisted and finally achieved great success. Often the biggest difference between the winners and the losers in the business world is persistence.

Still, persistence is no guarantee. Sometimes the best choice may be to pack up and go home. To quit or continue is one of the hardest decisions a businessperson ever faces. But here are some good rules of thumb. Walk away if your business has never been profitable and, realistically, it never will be. Walk away if your business only worked in unique circumstances—as with day-trading and flipping houses—that are unlikely to recur regularly in the future.

But persist, despite difficulties, if your business has worked under certain circumstances and those circumstances are likely to prevail in the future. For instance, hang in there if your growing cosmetic surgery practice sees a plunge in business because of a recession and a rash of scary news stories. Remember the trend. Millions of baby boomers are amassing more: (1) money and (2) wrinkles, liver spots, and saggy parts. They will spend a lot of 1 to get rid of 2.

Not long ago I asked a successful client what the most important ingredient to his success was. He did not hesitate: "I could not have done it without persistence." This was the key, he repeated: "persistence." That's the word from a guy who sold his software company and netted over $100 million.

Like every businessperson, he had had his share of trials and tribulations: lost contracts, lost employees, bad days. Even during the sale of his business, just as he was envisioning the millions of dollars he was about to receive, the deal nearly died—twice. But he never gave up.

Another successful client, a couple, fought off numerous challenges both large and small. They started out by buying a run-down hardware store and grew their business to nine stores in key locations throughout the city.

Along the way, a national chain moved in and pounded them with advertising and cutthroat pricing. All of their customers started insisting on more for less. The cost of labor jumped, when they could find good people. Rents skyrocketed.

Still, they persisted.

One day, one of the owners called in tears. Her heart was broken. She had just caught a longtime manager filling his car with merchandise stolen out of the back of the store. This from a guy they had hired out of high school and mentored up the company ladder—someone they had trusted and considered family. This betrayal took the heart out of them. It was the last thing they needed. But they kept on going.

After ten years of striving, their persistence finally paid off. A competitor had been making insultingly low buyout offers for years. As my client's chain of stores grew, this competitor became desperate for these locations. The competitor's offer finally skyrocketed.

My client gave me an ambitious target price, knowing there were no guarantees. They continued to run the business, struggling with customers and vendors and employees and landlords and lenders, as negotiations with the prospective buyer raged on.

Shortly after 8:00 P.M. on a Wednesday in the fall of 1997, they got the call. "We got a deal," I told them. They would get a multimillion-dollar payday, for even more than they had asked.

It took months to close on the sale, but soon they got the check that set them up for the rest of their lives. Here's the thing, though: We had a secret. On the day we struck the deal, the net worth of their company was seven dollars. Yes. Seven dollars. How could that be? The competition, the costs, and the cutthroat nature of the business had all taken a toll. They had dynamite locations and great revenues that were very valuable to the purchaser, but the till was empty. So many times it would have been easy for this couple to just give up. But they hung in there and won.

This is a marathon. Some days it's even going to seem like a triathlon, running in the Mojave, biking up Everest, and swimming in shark-infested waters. Focus on the finish line. The only way you'll get there is if you keep on trying.

Persistence pays.

# 8

## The Vision Thing

*Having One and Sharing It*

In the early 1990s, Freddy graduated from college. Barely.

Freddy had a dilemma. He wanted to get rich. But he didn't want to work hard. Certainly not like his dad, who owned a dry cleaners and worked the cash register from seven in the morning to seven at night. Not like his college buddies working for big accounting firms or ad agencies or going to law or med school.

Freddy asked around. No one was throwing money at lazy grads who minored in Fantasy Football.

But the Universe had a special purpose for Freddy. In college, Freddy had scored beer money scalping concert tickets. This, it turned out, was his calling. Freddy was the rain man of ticket scalping. He bought low. He sold high. He held his Springsteen tickets till the price peaked. He dumped his Vanilla Ice tickets before the plunge. So after college he went into the business full-time. He wasn't getting rich, but soon he was making as much as his buddies with "real" jobs.

But the business was work, work, work. Just selling two tickets could mean haggling to buy them, driving across town to pick them up, and then negotiating again on the phone to sell them: "I got two on the thirty-yard line. . . . Listen, these are hot tickets. You don't want them, I'll sell them to someone else. . . . Yeah, three hundred dollars for the pair. Take it or leave it. . . . Okay. Come by the office with cash and they'll be waiting for you." Next call. Same conversation. Freddy spent half of his time with a phone pressed to his ear. The rest of the time, he was managing the scalpers he hired, writing classified ads for upcoming events, or taking calls from customers complaining about bad seats. On game days he was outside the stadium in the bitter cold or sweltering heat, cutting more deals.

Still, Freddy loved the scalping business. He just wanted a better way to do it. Like every entrepreneur who hits a roadblock, he struggled with the question of how to change his business. He thought of switching advertising or hiring new people or opening a store or selling in other cities. But each of these ideas involved a lot of work and wouldn't make the business any easier.

Then, one day, it hit Freddy. He was dialing up his AOL account on one phone line and dealing with a wary customer on another. She was afraid to pay premium prices for what might be nosebleed seats. Freddy wished there was a seating chart in the sky that he could show her when he was jolted by the shrill screech of his modem connection. At that instant, it all crystallized. He should be selling his tickets on the World Wide Web.

Freddy envisioned a Web site where his customers could see the seats and the prices, buy his tickets, and quit bugging him. He would build his own Web site and scalp tickets on the Internet. Less work. More money. Hallelujah!

But remember, this was the early 1990s, so everyone thought he was crazy. Web sites didn't sell things then, except porn and fake pharmaceuticals. Legit businesses had just started dipping their toes into the Internet using "billboard" Web sites with pretty pictures that directed you to their brick-and-mortar stores.

Everywhere he went, he faced objection. Freddy's friends and family were concerned. Even his mom: "Freddy, you have such a good little business. Why mess with success? No one is going to buy things on that Interweb."

His employees absolutely hated the idea. "No one will trust a Web site with their credit card," one said. "People want to talk to a real human being when they are buying something," warned another. "And they want the tickets in their hands before they let go of their money." But Freddy understood. Mostly, his employees were afraid that they wouldn't be Top Dogs anymore. They were afraid of losing their jobs. They were afraid of change. It was like unveiling your new robot line at an AFL-CIO convention.

But Freddy believed in his vision. That's the thing about vision. When you have one, you are convinced—in your gut and your head—you have the right, new way to do business. You clearly see the path—all of the stepping-stones on a journey to success. It is not just an idea. It is a voyage that includes a destination at a new improved business—new for your company and sometimes even new for the world.

Understand, though, you might never have a vision. Not every entrepreneur has vision and not every successful business is driven by one. In fact, many of both do well without vision. They cover the basics, increase earnings every year, and attract buyers willing to pay a fortune. That's quite all right.

## Seeing Is Believing

There are also no instructions for getting visions. You either get one or you don't. It's like singing and painting. Picking up a paintbrush or a microphone won't make you an artist. I could take all the singing classes in the world and you would still throw eggs at me if I sang.

But when you do have vision, it propels the growth and sale of your business. It attracts people to your company, inspires them once they are part of your team, and reinforces them when times are tough.

**VISION ATTRACTS:** People want to be part of something bigger than themselves—like a movement. Vision changes a job into a mission. It's the difference between pouring coffee at Joe's Diner and Bringing Coffee to the World at Starbucks. A compelling vision attracts employees.

**VISION INSPIRES:** "One's reach should exceed one's grasp." Vision shows you are reaching to achieve some kind of new greatness. Your vision won't always be realistic. But it expands the aspirations of you and your colleagues. President John F. Kennedy shared a vision of putting a man on the moon. A decade of inspired achievement followed. People try harder when inspired.

**VISION REINFORCES:** A vision is also a mantra—a combination of fact and aspiration—that allows your team to group and regroup around a cause, especially in unsettled times. When you face challenges, vision will keep you stronger because it reminds you of what you are working to achieve.

If you have a vision for your business, here are a few pointers:

1. Get input. You may understand the path, but talking with others will illuminate the obstacles.

2. Keep in mind that if it's truly visionary, everyone will accept it as common wisdom—someday. In the meantime, you will need to overcome reluctant employees, conservative lenders, frightened spouses, and suspicious government officials.

3. Let people voice their objections. A lot of leaders are afraid that complaints will spread and strengthen. The opposite is usually true, especially if you meet privately and let people disagree. If they can vent, they are much more likely to put aside their objections.

4. Don't give up control over your vision. Businesses are not democracies. Neither is your vision.

5. Integrate your vision into your business plan. You will never achieve your vision if you don't have a plan for implementing it.

6. For the sake of credibility, show tangible progress. If you're going to put people on Mars in a decade, build a space station within a year or two. If you're Freddy, you'd better have a mock-up of the Web site ready for a staff meeting in a few months.

7. Don't get locked in. Let your vision evolve, not every day, but over time and especially with new developments.

8. Remember that because visionaries are often ahead of their time, they are also often ahead of the rules. Sometimes the law doesn't yet allow you to achieve your vision. You may have to lobby for new laws to do business—like the ones that now let people mail wine across the country.

## Living the Dream

Guided by his vision, Freddy proceeded to change the scalping world. He hired a software programmer and built his pioneering Web site. It showed the layout for each venue—you could see exactly where you were going to sit. You could see how many tickets were available and the price for each. You could pay for your tickets with a credit card. You could enter your address and the Web site knew exactly where to send your tickets—it even printed the mailing labels. Longer naps for Freddy! The Web site could sell thousands of tickets on the Internet with less cost and effort than selling ten tickets the old way.

It was like inventing fire or the wheel.

But all that change rocked his employees. Some had spent the last ten years building contacts and know-how that they feared would become worthless—just like a lot of employees feel around visionary businesses.

Freddy understood and calmed his team, in his own special way. "Quit your whining!" he barked. "No one's losing their jobs." Freddy explained that while they wouldn't be selling, there would be plenty of work buying tickets to feed Web site sales: "That's not bad; it's just different." To some, it was a slap in the face. But it was reality: "Listen, we've got plenty of competition. Our survival depends on staying ahead. If we don't sell on the Web, somebody will. Then we'll all be out jobs." That's when the employees rallied. They realized that they were much more likely to keep their jobs working for a Web site than competing against one.

For a while Freddy ran both the traditional scalping business and the Web site. But Web site sales zoomed. Soon customers were more comfortable dialing up the Web site than calling or buying in person. Most of his competitors were still sweating it out on street corners. But some joined Freddy and did quite well scalping tickets on the Web. One of them, StubHub, was purchased by eBay in 2007 for a reported $310 million.

And that's how Freddy and his vision helped revolutionize the ticket-selling business. He transformed his street-corner job scalping tickets into a multimillion-dollar Internet business. Not that any of this affected Freddy's challenged work ethic. To this day, if I call him and ask for tickets, he says, "Don't bug me. Go to the Web site."

# 9

## Values and Culture

### *Profit Rules*

M ost businesses say they are friendly places to work. A lot of firms like to say they're "collegial" (it's a big fifty-cent word). They leave out the fact that some of the partners don't talk to each other. Literally, they walk down the hall and look away from each other when they pass. Then there are the companies that go on about how much they care about their employees—and fire them when they get sick. Or take the companies that pay their executives millions of dollars per year but fire hundreds of workers when the executives screw up. When the executives really screw up, they get multimillion-dollar severance packages.

Most of us have worked at one of these dysfunctional companies. You didn't respect your boss or believe in your company. You weren't treated fairly and you didn't like the way they ran things. You didn't give them your best work. You didn't even like going to work. The best thing about the job was the ride home. When you worked there you were looking for a job somewhere else, and when you left you didn't refer any employees or new business to the company. You're probably still bad-mouthing them today.

What's wrong with these companies? Bad values and worse culture.

Most owners don't even consider the role of values and culture in the success of their business. They think about selling their televisions or landing a big contract or making a million bucks a year. Seeking success is fine. But people are not objects. There is a right way and a wrong way to treat people while you're building a business. The right way enriches your entire team.

For example, the typical entrepreneur worries too much about slicing the pie. "Are my employees getting too much? Am I getting too little?" Successful owners don't worry as much about the slicing. They make the pie bigger. How?

It all starts with the right values and culture.

Values are the rules your business lives by. Respect for others is a value. Fairness is a value. Keeping your word is a value. Your values are also reflected in the way you treat your employees, how you compensate them, what you reward and what you don't. The right values reinforce your system of doing business—your business model.

Culture is the environment you create when you live by your values. A caring, productive environment is a culture. So is a cutthroat, backstabbing environment. You have the power to create either one. The caring, productive culture takes a lot more work and discipline to achieve, but it's the best way to make money.

## Let's Not and Say We Did

Take the airlines. We used to enjoy flying; now we endure it. Flying has become such a miserable experience in large part because the airlines treat their own people terribly. Everyone I know has a horror story. Here's mine: I am flying back from Florida. My flight is canceled (no surprise there). I speak to the supervisor. You know the type, dingy short-sleeve shirt and dandruff in his mustache. He looks at me with weary, almost listless eyes and says, "I don't care. We don't care. None of us care. We are all just waiting till we can retire." How could I get mad at him? Obviously his company wasn't taking care of him. So little wonder that he was in no mood to take care of his customers.

If you treat your employees badly, they will leave or they will stay and sabotage your company. The first to leave will often be the most talented. Sadly, the ones who stay are usually your least capable. They can't get a job anywhere else. These "stranded" employees certainly aren't in a mood to treat your customers very well. Think "Do unto others."

One company I worked with—call them Dysfunctional Professionals, PC—was owned by a trio of talented professionals but had poor morale and could never grow. Their best employees left with alarming regularity. They invited me to observe their operations and diagnose the problems that had been crippling them for years.

It only took one meeting to see the problem: Selfish Owners and Bosses—SOBs for short.

DysPro held regular "all-hands" meetings that were intended to improve morale. How ironic. Ostensibly, the meetings would clear the air by allowing employees to air grievances and also giving them an opportunity to offer up ideas for improving the company. Yet another road paved with good intentions. At the meeting I attended, one employee expressed concerns about the health insurance benefits the company provided. But one partner hadn't yet shown up and another was wandering into the meeting as the employee spoke. Next, an employee had an idea for improving company productivity. By then, the partners were reading e-mails on their BlackBerrys and goofing off in the back of the room, looking up every now and then to see if it was their turn to talk. Another employee suggested a new way to use the company computers to improve customer service. Still the owners weren't listening and didn't respond to any suggestions. These employees might as well have been talking to my dog. At least he would have wagged appreciatively.

The DysPro partners went to the "lip service" school of respect for their employees. They said they cared about their employees. Otherwise, why have the meetings in the first place? But who's kidding who? Showing up late, walking in and out of the meeting, reading your e-mails, goofing off, and ignoring your colleagues—it all says: "I don't care."

Like many people, the partners were unduly self-centered. This preoccupation with their own needs hurt the partners and their company. Their employees felt frustrated and rejected. Some got angry and left. Others stayed and grew bitter. The partners often would train promising employees for a year or two only to find that they grew disillusioned and quit. Yet there is a certain justice about selfish company values—you rarely profit from them.

When it comes to values, you have to talk the talk *and* walk the walk. Just saying your company has values doesn't work. It's the difference between *stated* values and *actual* values. For instance, a company might claim they respect the needs of their customers and yet keep them in long lines or on hold or locked in planes that are stuck on the ground without working bathrooms or food, water, or clean air. Does a medical conglomerate really care about you if it leaves you waiting for the doctor, sitting naked on a sheet of paper, for thirty minutes in a cold room? Look at Circuit City. In March of 2007, it fired thirty-four hundred of its highest-paid employees and hired cheaper workers in an attempt to cut costs and boost profits. This shortsighted move backfired—almost immediately. As *The Washington Post* reported, the company posted losses of $80 million to $90 million for the first quarter of its 2008 fiscal year because of "substantially below-plan sales," especially of televisions. Perhaps you can't sell complicated big-screen televisions with rookies. As we all know now, it didn't take long before Circuit City filed for bankruptcy and went out of business.

## You've Lost That Loving Feeling

Some companies have bad values. They don't even know or try and end up with whatever values are spawned by knee-jerk reactions to life. Other companies start off on the right foot. The owners are sincere. They brainstorm about the right values, draw up a list, and then commit to live by it. Then good intentions crash into real-world pressures or old bad habits surface. You see that a lot.

One law firm I know used to pay the attorneys—the associates, not the partners—haphazardly, with no real rules. If an associate brown-nosed or socialized with a boss, maybe he got more. Eventually, the partners stumbled onto an old, traditional law firm formula that aligned the firm's values—the rules they lived by—with their goals, boosting their success, both short and long term. The partners collected the revenues each associate generated and kept a third for themselves, applied a third to overhead, and gave a third to the associate in the form of salary and bonuses. If the associates worked long and hard and kept the clients happy, the firm generated a lot of revenues and the associates earned more bonuses and were inspired to work harder. Conversely, if a client was dissatisfied—maybe an associate's work was late or sloppy—then the client didn't pay or demanded a discount. So the associate got feedback—the kind you feel in the wallet—that encouraged not just a lot of work, but prompt, quality work. By sharing the rewards of good work, the partners encouraged better performance by their associates and reinforced the firm's business model of providing quality, timely service.

It was a simple, successful formula. The associates loved it, because they could almost count the dollars in their pockets as they worked. They could spend a Saturday in the office and imagine the Redskins tickets they would buy. They could work late every night for a few weeks and pay for a vacation with the bonus. The partners got a third of everything as compensation for the early days when they were building the firm and didn't make a lot of money. All was well.

The formula was successful, but it wasn't perfect. It gave associates a slice of the pie and thereby a sense of ownership, but there were drawbacks. Attorneys could work so hard that they burned out. And there was no incentive for an attorney to do anything he couldn't bill for, like mentoring or pro bono work. Overall, though, this compensation system reinforced values that produced a successful, well-oiled business machine.

Then the partners got greedy and threw sand in the gears. They didn't just want their fair share; they wanted to take off early every

Friday, play golf, and make more money than ever. So they decided that their most successful associates were making too much and couldn't make more than $110,000 per year—which meant a pay cut for the best performers. Certainly, the partners reasoned, this was still a lot of money and "in their day" they toiled far harder for far less. Moreover, they gleefully reminded each other, the less the associates made, the more for the partners.

Well, pigs get fed and hogs get slaughtered. Oh, sure, for the first few months the new system did seem to "work." The associates continued their past level of high performances, sheerly on momentum. The partners kept more of the revenues than they ever had before. But under the new rules, that meant less money for the associates. The geniuses behind the curtain never predicted that their top associates would quickly—nay, immediately—realize that no matter how hard they worked, their pay was capped. Before long, these star associates reined in their efforts, began looking at employment ads, talking with recruiters, and going on interviews. These best and brightest discovered they would make more money elsewhere. And so they did. Go elsewhere.

The firm lost its golden geese to other law firms, often to longstanding rivals. It's probably no surprise which attorneys stuck around. It was the people who weren't very talented or hardworking and simply couldn't find work elsewhere. The greedy partners implemented a value system that drove off their best associates and retained the worst. The partners failed to align the values of their business with their business model of attracting and retaining talented attorneys and inspiring them to produce a lot of high-quality work. The best way for a star associate to make more money was to leave the business!

Time-out. Some of you have to be thinking that these partners couldn't be this shortsighted, that Jack must be making this up. No, this really happened. It happens all over America—all of the time.

Consider the sales manager who says—and I have heard this counterproductive statement all too many times—"None of my salespeople are going to make more money than me!" Well, if you are the world's best salesperson and your boss doesn't make too much money, this rule is certainly going to drive you away.

True story: Biggest sale ever in the history of a small software company. What did they do for their persistent, risk-taking salesman who knocked on the door of the Department of Defense a hundred times until they finally let him in and made a deal? Give him a parade? A medal? A celebratory dinner? Nope, they fired him. As in, "Here's a box. Get your stuff. Good knowing you." Why boot their superhero salesman? The geniuses running this company simply wanted to avoid paying him the commission. Honestly, they were that ~~stupid~~ short-sighted. So let's score this move. We have a small company with two critical components to its business model: first, good software, and second, motivated people selling it. What did they win? They saved some money in the short term, in a rather despicable way, by not paying a commission. What did they lose? They sabotaged their business model by killing the morale of their remaining salespeople. Who is going to be knocking on doors for them in the future?

## Walking the Walk

Successful companies align their value systems with their business model. These companies pay, reward, and promote employees for fulfilling company values.

One client, Leigh, told me about the values that drove his company's success.

1. Our company takes care of our employees.

2. In turn, our employees will take care of our customers.

3. When our employees take care of our customers, our customers naturally will take care of our company with more business—which, by the way, provides the money we need to continue to take care of our employees.

Leigh didn't just talk the talk. Sure, he provided ample benefits. Yes, he trained and nurtured his employees, allowing them to grow into positions of increasing responsibility and compensation. But in a spectacular display of commitment to his values and his employees, Leigh created a "share-the-wealth" program—technically, called a Unit Appreciation Rights program. This UAR program gave hundreds of employees an opportunity to earn a piece of the pie if and when the company was sold. The program gave employees more money based on their performance. For example, you got more if you were part of a team that won a new contract or expanded business with an existing customer. Employees also received more money the longer they stayed with the company. And if you quit, you got nothing.

Leigh was generous. But this wasn't charity—far from it. The UAR program was good business. His employees worked harder, improving company performance. They stayed longer, reducing turnover costs. Better yet, when really tough times hit—and boy, did they hit, with lost contracts, stalled growth, and falling revenues—his employees did not abandon ship. They knew that if they hung in there and fought through the difficulties, they would share millions of dollars.

One employee, Frank, was a perfect example. Leigh had hired Frank twenty years earlier, when the company was a couple of years old, operating out of a warehouse with a handful of employees. Frank had just graduated from a top college, was a brilliant guy, and could have worked anywhere. In fact, he was completely overqualified for a job with this shaky start-up. A small business normally wouldn't have attracted Frank and certainly would have lost him later to a better-paying or more prestigious job. But, because of Leigh's commitment to take care of his employees, to share the wealth, and to do the right thing, Frank did join Leigh—and stayed. Frank went on to win numerous major contracts for the company, led teams that ran the biggest projects for the company's most valuable customers, and helped grow the company to sales of over $200 million per year. True to their values, Frank worked his way up the ladder and became company President.

Leigh, Frank, and the rest of the team made it all work. In February 2006, Leigh sold the business for well over $100 million. Then, as promised, Leigh gave $40 million to his employees, in payments ranging from $10,000 to millions per employee.

Now, that's walking the walk.

This $40 million didn't just drop into the laps of the employees. Leigh created a company that cared. For twenty-plus years, the company grew under Leigh's values and the culture they established, until you had two hundred people all rowing hard and in unison toward a common goal. They all shared a vision. Every day the team worked hard to make their company a success and that dream a reality.

Frank? He got more than $5 million, plus a great job, benefits, and stock options with the new owner.

## Building the Right Values and Culture

How do you pick the right values? How do you create a successful culture? Practicing the following could save your company's life:

- You reinforce what you reward. So reward the behavior that you want to encourage.

- Following company values should guide advancement within the company. Promote those who follow, not flout, your values.

- Positive reinforcement works. Punishment doesn't. If you are resorting to punishment, something major is broken. Step back and rethink things.

- Money is not the only reward. Provide your team members with recognition of achievements and increasing responsibility.

- Say "thank you." Mean it.

- Leaders lead. Leaders lead by example. The owners and officers of the company must follow the rules. Nothing undermines a rule more than when a leader ignores it.

It is not nearly as hard as you might think. Almost all of us know the right thing to do. The challenge is having the discipline to do it.

# 10

## Overcoming Self-Destructiveness

*Your Worst Enemy*

W e've all caused those embarrassing situations when we say the exact wrong thing precisely at the worst possible moment. You know the feeling, so cringe inducing that your blood pressure spikes and you start sweating just by thinking about it. It happens to all of us on occasion; just ask anyone who has had a few too many drinks at a party. But if it occurs with regularity, especially when you're running your company, then you have a problem. It's called self-destructive behavior—and it's ruined everyone from the owner of the mom-and-pop pizza shop who refuses to get the proper permits to the chairman of the Fortune 50 company who buys six-thousand-dollar shower curtains on the company tab and ends up in jail.

We're all human, so we all have issues. But self-destructive behavior sinks businesses. Take, for example, one entrepreneur I worked with who had a case so extreme, he could teach Martha Stewart a few lessons. (After all, did the domestic diva really need to save money on insider-trading deals?) We'll call our guy Henry, Hank for short.

Even though Hank's business card identified him as a real estate broker, most people referred to him in less flattering terms. Maybe because he once announced—loudly—at an employee's wedding reception, "I've never seen an uglier wedding party." Then there was the time he bought booze for some of his underage workers and helped them load it into their cars as they left work for the weekend. Let's not forget Hank's frequent outbursts at work. While none of them have sued (yet), he has strangled four different employees (and counting). Maybe Hank is just frustrated at his inability to fire his least productive workers—his sons and his wife, whom he never should have hired in the first place. The world might think Hank is a jerk, but in reality he's troubled and lost and doesn't know what to do about it. In the end, he lost his business.

It shouldn't take a Ph.D. to realize Hank is incredibly self-destructive. But while it's easier to see this behavior in its most extreme forms, most business leaders fail—or refuse—to see it in themselves. If you need examples, just check the headlines. Self-destructive behavior explains why:

- A powerful U.S. congressman sends career-ending instant messages to pages.

- Countless heads of publicly traded companies, each earning tens of millions of dollars a year, accept backdated stock options or trade on insider information or outright loot their company.

- An NFL star is forced to give up millions—and the limelight—because he won't give up pot.

Tragically, Len Bias died using drugs just after being picked second overall in the first round of the 1986 NBA draft. U.S. presidents have lost or jeopardized their enormous power for petty crimes and misdemeanors. And our country's minimum-security prisons are filled with onetime executive superstars who allowed their self-destruction compulsions to rob them of everything. In every case, the culprit snatched defeat from the jaws of victory.

Self-destruction claims many victims, and it could be destroying—or severely hampering—you and your business. How can you tell? Take a look at these common symptoms and decide if any seem familiar.

- You're never able to go beyond a certain level of success.

- You consistently make mistakes that hurt your business, and worse yet, they're the exact same mistakes.

- Your good employees are quitting and you can't get rid of the bad ones.

- You engage in behavior or language at work that makes your employees and clients uncomfortable.

- You tell risqué jokes and not everyone laughs.

- You take risks you shouldn't, like breaking the law, which could have dire consequences for your company (and we're not talking about speeding on empty highways).

- You break your word to others, sometimes your solemn word—as in cheating on your spouse or business partner.

- You're jealous of—sometimes even paralyzed by—the success of others.

- You're unable to make key decisions.

- You're late for important meetings and you miss key deadlines.

- You drink away your problems.

- You frequently wonder, "How did I get in this situation, again?"

The symptoms are evident in the way you operate your business. Do you constantly hire the wrong employees or fail to effectively communicate with your team? Do you send your employees on wild-goose chases or take your eye off the ball of your primary business objectives? How well do you handle your budget? Ever been guilty of allocating money on high-risk, low-reward ventures? Do you allow your emotions to cause you to spend cash on vindictive lawsuits instead of focusing on the future? Speaking of the future, do you really work for success and have a plan ready for setbacks? If you said "yes" to many of these questions, then you're well aware how self-destructiveness undermines ambitions, careers, and companies.

When your problems consistently hurt your business—and your life—then you need help. I understand that admitting you have problems isn't easy. I know. I, too, have confronted issues that I had previously long ignored.

Here's the reality. People come to me for legal work and business strategy—but they bring their baggage with them. Their business concerns may fill the conversation, but their self-destructive behavior is a cloud that hangs over the room. It frustrates our game plan at every turn. This self-destructiveness is just another problem affecting their business goals, and we need to deal with it. I wouldn't be doing my job if I didn't bring it to my clients' attention. Now here's the problem. They don't believe or want to believe they have psychological problems or there even is something called self-destructiveness. I have seen people lose the deal of a lifetime all due to self-inflicted wounds and point to every reason under the sun except to their own self-destructive behavior. The unfortunate reality is that most entrepreneurs perceive their psychological issues as they do Pandora's box: a matter best left closed.

When I raise the subject, however delicately, some entrepreneurs are receptive, some must be tricked, and some only respond to a dire crisis.

It took Mark, one of my clients, the umpteenth loss of a valued employee to realize how dysfunctional his behavior was. "Jack, I'm through," Mark said in a voice cracking with emotion. Normally reserved to a fault, he asked, "Why won't people work for me? Betty just quit. Paul just gave his notice. Neither of them have jobs to go to. They just say it's too stressful to work here. Without them, I don't think I can go on. I'm not sleeping. I'm not eating. Half the time I'm sitting at my desk getting nothing done. I'm ready to walk away, too."

"Mark," I asked, "what if we could change all that? What if I could show you things that would make your company more successful and more profitable?"

"Sign me up!" Mark chuckled, his first laugh in weeks. "What do I have to do?"

Even with his newfound enthusiasm, I have learned to introduce the solution slowly. Great change begins with small steps.

The solution is counseling, which I euphemistically refer to as "coaching," "consulting," "business counseling," or "counseling," depending on the trepidation of my clients. It's one thing to do it; it's another to tell them what we're doing or, worse yet, hit them over the head with it. Some are just too threatened and scared to admit they need a shrink. Many would rather self-destruct. So, most often, I introduce them to a qualified "consultant" who, as part of our team, can help them address our concerns. I work with business psychologists because they're trained in dealing with the issues entrepreneurs face. Just like sports psychologists know how to help golfers get over the "yips," these specialists understand the pressures of the business world.

What causes people to be self-destructive, and how do we help? The experts I've worked with have explained that self-destructive behavior often is the product of a lack of feelings of self-worth that takes root very early in one's life. At its core, this low self-esteem is caused by improper parenting and inappropriate behavior by important figures in our lives. Most likely, your parents and others did their best. But all too often, their best was hand-me-downs of poor parenting skills. Bottom line: we sabotage ourselves because we believe we don't deserve success.

How do I help? With knowledgeable "consultants," my clients and I begin the process of recognizing the problem. From there, we work on avoiding self-destructive behavior.

Later we delve deeper into why my clients generate self-destructive behavior in the first place. Ultimately, they replace their low self-esteem with a healthy self-image. Don't get me wrong. I understand most people think this is mumbo jumbo. My own brother thinks "self-destructiveness" is a made-up word. But I know it exists. All you have to do is open your eyes. I like to say people have an internal thermostat for success and happiness. They allow themselves to reach a certain level, but if they go over it, they'll do something self-destructive to bring themselves back to their "setting." The counseling process involves replacing pathological thinking that tells us "we're bad" with the understanding that we are essentially good, but we all have our problems and need to work on them. In short, as we progress, we reset the thermostat at increasingly higher levels. Each new setting brings progress. Clients start making better decisions, and their relationships improve both at work and at home.

For Dan, one of my clients, every day was like riding a bucking horse. He was bruised and battered from being thrown on a regular basis. He had employees berating him for his inconsistent management and had vital workers threatening to quit because the rotten apples were getting away with murder. On top of that, he had partners who failed to share in the responsibilities, when they weren't undermining his leadership. If he hadn't paid so much to buy in, he would have walked away. But there was one bright spot. He knew he needed help. He asked me for that help. A breakthrough came when I was presenting a new employment manual to his staff. One of the rotten apples challenged me, offended by the concept of showing up for work on time. She asked why the employees should accept new rules that would take away their rights. But instead of being combative, I explained to her how the new rules would actually make her life easier—by balancing the workload more evenly. "It's going to give, not take away," I told her. "If everyone shows up on time and does their job, than no one has to do their own work and someone else's, too."

Dan was struck by my confidence. He said, "Jack, I want to be able to handle my employees like you do. I would have been angry when she asked that question. Instead you were calm and cool. What's your secret?"

Dan began seeing a business shrink. The first baby steps involved rewarding good behavior at work and avoiding hiring bad employees. As Dan's self-confidence increased, he began successfully addressing sensitive subjects, not just with his partners but also at home and elsewhere. As he improved, his employees joined him. Many took him up on his offer to let them see the company shrink. But others fled, too threatened by what they might find out about themselves. That was also helpful, because it forced out the bad apples. To this day, the company owner continues with periodic counseling, as do many of his colleagues. Dissention has declined. The business is healthier and happier. Productivity and profits have increased.

Your issues are like splinters. You can leave them in or dig them out. Endless pain or an end to pain? Your choice.

# 11

# Inc., LLC, or Partnership

## *The Right Structure for Your Business*

Harold and his brother Tommy should have felt like Bill Gates, not frustrated bank robbers. After all, they had built a profitable business selling fuel to independent gas stations. Sure, there were headaches. That's normal. The beauty was, their company threw off a reliable stream of cash. Even better, they finally received that dream offer to sell that would let them both retire comfortably. But just like the bandits who found out the bills were marked and couldn't be spent, Harold and Tommy discovered a big problem that killed the deal.

Yes, these guys were geniuses when it came to fuel. They understood how to buy fuel, how to price it, and how to sell it. They locked up supply when prices were low and steadily expanded by underpricing the competition.

But they were no experts in setting up a business. They didn't even know what they didn't know. They just followed their friends. Harold and Tommy went online, clicked a smiley-face icon, and paid $129 for their very own corporation. They got fancy stock certificates, a fake leather notebook embossed with the company name in gold print, and a seal that made impressive patterns on the documents they signed. They got a letter from the state telling them they were incorporated. They loved their new business name—the way "Inc." looked at the end of "Acme Fuels." Harold was older, so he got to be President.

Tommy, the younger brother, was delighted to be Vice President. They thought they were on the ultimate path to cashing out.

When it really counted, though, that path led right off a cliff.

The offer to sell was great. But the amount they would put in their pockets wasn't. To their amazement, their big payoff would be chewed up in taxes. First, Acme Fuels, Inc., would get clobbered with a ginormous tax on the sale of the business. Then, when Harold and Tommy got what was left, they would get walloped again with taxes. Same sale, double the taxation. This double taxation would cost them more than half of the profits on the sale of their business. Not exactly the American Dream. Reluctantly, they decided not to sell—and they continued to turn down offers for the same reason.

Worst of all, this double taxation would have been easy to avoid. Simply put, they didn't pick the right structure for their business. What does this mean and why is it important?

## Pick the Right Entity

Having the right structure for your business is like having the right house for your family. First, you need to pick the right type of building. You wouldn't want to live in a warehouse or an office building. In business this building is called an entity, and you will be picking from a variety of entities. You have probably already heard of the leading entities in America today:

- Corporations

- Subchapter S corporations

- Partnerships

- Limited liability companies (LLCs)

Each of these types of entities offers different advantages and disadvantages, such as:

**NO PERSONAL LIABILITY:** If you're personally liable and your business fails to pay its bills or breaks its agreements, others can sue you personally and take your house, your car, and the shirt right off your back. Protection against personal liability is one of the most important things you can get from setting up your business right. To continue with the house analogy, avoiding personal liability is like having a good shelter against storms. Some entities, especially corporations, provide great protection against personal liability. Corporations are like castles with a moat protecting owners and their assets from lawsuits.

However, when you don't form any entity for your business, you are operating as a "sole proprietorship" and exposing yourself to full personal liability. You have no shelter at all. It's like living in a tent and only appropriate where you have little risk or little to lose. This is fine if you're twelve years old and you deliver newspapers, cut lawns, or shovel snow. Outside of these critical areas of commerce (I know, they were my first three jobs), stay away from sole proprietorships.

**TRANSFERABILITY:** If you want to raise money to start or grow your business, you need the ability to give investors a piece of the company. This ability to transfer ownership interests in your company, such as stock, is called transferability. Transferability is also important when you want to divvy up ownership of the business among the co-founders or offer employees the prospect of ownership. Corporations and LLCs allow you to freely transfer stock—in an LLC, stock is called membership interests. However, Subchapter S corporations put a stranglehold on the number and type of owners in your company, choking off your ability to raise money from investors.

**FLEXIBILITY:** Owning an interest in a business often comes down to money and control. Some people care more about the cash, others more about the power. One gal might want a guaranteed dividend and as long as she gets it, she doesn't care who's running the show. Another guy might be a control freak, wanting the right to approve every deal and every hire. The ability to distribute rights to money and control among the owners is "flexibility." Again, Subchapter S corporations strait-jacket you. Regular corporations and partnerships offer plenty of wiggle room. But LLCs free you to cut almost any deal you can imagine. Let's say you have one investor who is borrowing money to buy an interest in your company. But she's anxious about her ability to repay the borrowed funds to her bank. You can't guarantee her that you will be successful, but you can entice her with a guarantee that she will get first dibs on the LLC's earnings. For those who want control in your LLC you can provide anything from a permanent role as co-manager of the business to a veto over major decisions.

There are plenty of other pros and cons to the entity you choose. Depending on the entity, you will have greater or lesser ability to:

- Provide tax-free fringe benefits, such as health insurance, to owner-employees

- Deduct business losses from owners' personal income taxes

- Use favorable accounting methods

- Reduce your taxes in a variety of ways

When Harold and Tommy set up their company, they should have talked to an expert. Because they ultimately wanted to sell their business, the expert would have warned them against forming a corporation. Instead, the expert would have recommended that they set up an LLC. An LLC would provide a variety of benefits, but most important, it would have let Harold and Tommy avoid double taxation on their profits when they sold. The company, Acme Fuels LLC, wouldn't be taxed at all. Instead, Harold and Tommy would personally pay taxes—just one time—on the profits they received from the sale of the business.

They also could have avoided double taxation by filing a simple form with the IRS. By filing this form when they first set up their corporation, Harold and Tommy could have elected to convert Acme Fuels, Inc., to a Subchapter S corporation. This election would eliminate that first layer of taxes on the company, just like with an LLC.

You may be wondering why Harold and Tommy didn't fix the double-taxation problem once they realized they had one. Unfortunately, some problems—like bedbugs—are a lot easier to avoid than they are to fix. Harold and Tommy finally made that Subchapter S election. But because they didn't do it when they first set up the company, the law requires them to wait ten years to avoid the double taxation.

The point isn't the particulars—it's the process. You need to pick the right structure for your company, and it takes expert advice to do that. You shouldn't expect to know all of the legal, tax, and accounting "ins and outs" of setting up your company the right way. What works for other business owners might not work for you. Also, this stuff is not common sense or a matter of gut instincts. It's about rules and technicalities—with expensive consequences when you guess wrong.

*Hard Way Rule #1:* When setting up your company, consult with experts, consider the pros and cons of each alternative, and pick the type of entity that will meet your short- and long-term goals.

Once you pick the right entity, you're not done. You need to set it up correctly. What that involves depends on the entity and who owns your company. Different things are required for each type of entity and, generally, the more owners you have, the more that is required.

## Get Your Agreements Right the First Time.

Darrell looked at the check in his hand. There were zeroes missing. All he knew was that he had worked for thirty years building a home-theater business with his ex–best friend, Ritchie. But when Darrell got in a car accident and couldn't work anymore, Ritchie bought him out based on an agreement they struck when they first started out together in business. That left Darrell holding a check with six figures when there should have been eight.

The sad fact was that Darrell got everything he bargained for. Problem was, he struck a bad bargain. Like a lot of people, when he and his partner started their business, they didn't want to waste their money on paperwork. Instead they wanted track lighting and a shag carpet in the display room. And they certainly didn't want to think through all those miserable "what if one of you dies" and "what if you two can't agree" scenarios their lawyer kept harping about. Thinking about who was going to buy out the other and for how much was worse than writing a will, for heaven's sake!

People want things simple even when things aren't. Darrell and Ritchie were no different. They didn't want to spend the money or time working through a complicated agreement. They would do a better agreement later. Sure.

That's like asking your spouse to sign a prenup years into the marriage. Think about it. You've been married for a decade or two. You're having the fight of your lives. You just said stuff you can never take back. So did your spouse. One of you is ready to storm out of the house and the other wants to break stuff. Does this sound like a good time to negotiate a prenup?

The same goes for your business. You need a good agreement from the outset. It is not enough to have an "agreement." You are not just checking an item off your "to do" list when you enter into one of these things. This is important. A bad agreement always benefits someone. Sure, *you* might be willing to change it later, even if this bad agreement benefits you. But your partners might not, especially if they have the advantage. It is just plain human nature.

Likewise, you don't want a simple agreement for a complex situation. People always think that they are starting out simple, so they can have a simple agreement. But even if it starts simple, business gets complex, and there is no magic moment when you and your partners huddle in the conference room and say, "Hey, we need that complex agreement we've been putting off." It just doesn't happen.

So *before* you invest your money, your brainpower, and all those days and years of hard work in a business, you and your partners need to draft an agreement that addresses all of the major issues and likely possibilities. It's the Bible for your business. It covers who controls the business, when money gets distributed, who does the hiring and fir- ing, and what happens if you and the other owners don't agree on how to run the company. It determines what happens if one of the owners is disabled, dies, or divorces. It also decides when one owner buys out the other, for how much, and when this amount is paid. A good agree- ment does all this and more.

The most important word in that last paragraph was "before" (as in "he got the antidote *before* he died").

But when Darrell and Ritchie started out in business, they did keep their agreement simple. Too simple, it turns out. They didn't want to go through all the brain damage, especially trying to figure out the right way to value the company. So instead they agreed the buyout price would be one-half of the "book value" of the company. They were told that it would be easy for their accountant to figure out the book value and there wouldn't be any disputes on how to calculate it. They thought they had a good, simple solution.

Well, it was simple. But it was not good. Book value grossly under- values most businesses. Book value essentially means the amount of your cash on hand plus the "yard sale" value of your assets. You know, the couch sells for two dollars and the lamp for fifty cents. That's an exaggeration, but you get the point. Book value is like sucker value or "the door was open, so I thought it was all free" value. You could have a business that a stranger would buy for tens of millions of dollars and yet the book value might only be a few hundred thousand dollars. No kidding. Book value puts no value on your brand, your goodwill in the community, or the fact that customers keep coming back. But Darrell didn't care about a buyout when he and Ritchie were drafting their agreement. Selling his interest in the company was just some abstract idea that was far off in the future.

As the years went by, however, Darrell realized that because he was older than Ritchie, Darrell was more likely to retire first. There would be a day he would be relying on their buyout formula. So every now and then, Darrell tried to get Ritchie to sit down and write up a new agreement, one that would accurately value their company. Ritchie refused. Maybe Ritchie knew he had the better end of an unfair deal.

And their buyout formula was unfair. The company's book value was paltry because they had a few floor models but no inventory to speak of and they leased all of their stores. When they had excess cash, they took it. Even though they had a business that would sell for tens of millions of dollars on the open market, the book value was only a few hundred thousand dollars.

So Darrell only got whiplash and a concussion in the car accident, but he got killed in the buyout.

*Hard Way Rule #2:* When you start out in business, having an agreement with your partners is not required by law. That's too bad, because it misleads folks. They enter into agreements that are too simple or just plain bad. That's always going to hurt at least one of you. And anyone who benefits isn't likely to the change the deal. You've only got one certain chance to get it right—at the beginning.

## Maintain the Proper Records

Have you ever been in an argument and you put your hands on the exact e-mail that shows you're right and your opponent is not only a liar but also an absolute idiot? Remember the satisfaction?

What wouldn't we all give for an "I'm right" form that we could wave in front of the motor vehicle administration or our health insurance company or someone suing us?

Well, when it comes to your business entity, you can have it. In fact, you're jeopardizing your business if you don't. As I discussed before, your business entity is like your house. You need to maintain it. If you don't clean the gutters, caulk the tiles, or change the filters, you're going to end up with big problems eventually. Ask my wife. I politely shouted the same insights at her after the rec room ceiling fell on my head. Apparently, when the upstairs bathtub overflows you need to mop, not let it evaporate!

The same goes for your business. It is not enough to pick the right entity (Hard Way Rule #1) and prepare the right agreements (Hard Way Rule #2). If you stop there, it could still all fall on your head. You need to maintain your entity. It's all part of keeping your house in order. The owners and officers need to meet periodically, document decisions, file reports, and record transactions. For instance, when you sell stock, you need to record it in the stock ledger. Likewise, when you lend money to an owner of the company, you need to have the borrower sign a promissory note and enter the loan in the company's books. When you change your name or start business in another state, you need to file the proper paperwork with the government. This diligent housekeeping will generate plenty of "I'm Right" forms on the way to growing and selling your company.

Consider what bad housekeeping could do to your company:

- You forget to file the personal property return for your corporation and overlook the warning notice from your state. As a result, you forfeit your corporate charter. Now you have no corporation and no shield protecting your business assets. You and the other owners of the company are personally liable for all company obligations until you magically "find" the necessary records, file your return, and pay the taxes, fines, and interest. It gets worse. Until you fix this mess, you are also in violation of your bank loan and many of your contracts. You're also disqualified from doing business with numerous parties, such as the government.

- You're meeting Agent Thick Brain from the IRS and you can't prove half of your deductions because you don't have expense records and can't document the business purpose of most of your travel, meal, and entertainment expenses. This won't kill your business, but it will increase your tax bill and reduce your ability to grow.

- You catch one of your partners stealing from the business. He denies everything and claims he was just borrowing from the company. You can't prove much. You never kept any records of your meetings. You never even documented loans to owners. Your lawyer warns you that you've got a horrible case. You're stuck with a thief for a partner unless you want to buy him out. If you had done the basic housekeeping, he'd be leaving with handcuffs, not a buyout.

- You're selling your business and your sloppy record keeping comes back to haunt you. The buyer is doing his due diligence and wants to see everything. In our house analogy, this is like the home inspection by the buyer before settlement. When you bring out the shopping bag of crumpled, jumbled company records, the sales price immediately drops 5 percent. The disgusted buyer even threatens to call off the sale altogether. Whether it's your home or company, a lack of long-term maintenance will ding you when it comes time to sell.

*Hard Way Rule #3:* Maintaining your entity is easy to ignore. It always seems like you have more important things to do. But in the long run, that lack of maintenance will build up and come back to haunt you. If you don't want that figurative roof falling down on your head, if you don't want to lose battles and devalue your business, you have to maintain it. And when you're in that win-or-lose situation, wouldn't you rather have a "gotcha" than be stung by one?

## There's More

A lot more. A painful amount more.

But this chapter is not about every nut and bolt on how to pick, document, and maintain the right entity for your business. There are whole books and plenty of lawyers, accountants, and other experienced advisors to tell you how to do it the right way. This chapter is all about having the motivation and process to get and keep your entity right.

So determine whether you should set up a corporation, partnership, or limited liability company:

- While you may have heard of these entities, you likely don't know how they really work. Don't let that stop you. Your job is to get the right experts in front of you and make good decisions based on their advice.

- Remember, a sole proprietorship is not an entity. Pick the right entity. Or do nothing. Wait to get sued.

Set up your entity correctly:

- You'll need an agreement among the owners whenever there are two or more of you (except a husband and wife who are comfortable relying on divorce laws to sort out the really big disagreements).

- These agreements are not legally required to create your entity. That's unfortunate. Because they are technically "extra," many people don't prepare them or don't spend enough time and effort on them. In this regard, starting a business is like starting a car. You can get moving if you know how to turn the key, put the car in drive, and hit the gas. But if you don't want to crash, you also need to know how to work the brakes, the windshield wipers, and a few of the other "extras."

- These agreements are hard to do right. You have to face some difficult issues. It is tempting to just say that you will deal with those issues later, if and when problems arise. But all too often that leaves you trying to write the rule book at the very time people don't agree and you need to be reading from an established rule book.

Maintain it properly:

- Just like it sounds, keep your house in order if you don't want it to crumble on you.

When people don't follow these rules and their business fails, anybody can sue them personally and take all their stuff. When their business is a success, they still have problems. They often end up in disputes with everyone around them—like former best friends fighting over a winning lottery ticket.

Don't learn these lessons the hard way.

# 12

## Financial Reports and Forecasts

*Where You've Been, How You're Doing,*

*and Where You're Going*

Sam didn't even know his mortgage business was dead. He was still fat and happy because there was money in the bank and loan requests rolling in. It was year-end and his company had brokered a few billion dollars' worth of loans—double the prior year's tally. Friends, family, strangers, and acquaintances were all refinancing and buying homes while rates were low. He didn't know that the money in the bank would soon belong to his creditors and the phone was about to stop ringing.

Sam had a finance department—if you want to call it that. Mostly, they paid bills and deposited checks. Like too many companies, the few financial reports they produced were way too late. Sam didn't know whether he made a profit or lost money in January until he finally got the monthly statement in April or May. He could only guess as to whether he should be hiring or firing or whether he should cut his advertising budget or ramp it up. And those reports only told him what had happened months ago. He had no system at all to tell him what was happening now or to give him an early warning of what would happen next. He didn't know if housing starts were up or down, whether refinancings were about to jump or decline, or whether all those first-time buyers were paying their subprime loans. He was running his business by hunch.

If Sam's business was a car and he was the driver, he was speeding down the highway with no dashboard and a windshield that was painted over. The only way Sam could tell if he was still on the road was a cracked rearview mirror that kept falling down on the floor. In the end, Sam totaled the car and ended up in a ditch. But he wouldn't have crashed his business if he had the financial systems to tell him where he had been, how he was doing, and where he was going.

As you grow your business, you need to produce the financial reports and forecasts that will tell you whether your company is worth more or less than it was before, whether you're making more money, or losing it and whether demand is growing or shrinking. Again, if your business is a car, you need a rearview mirror to tell where you've been (revenues and expenses, assets and liabilities), a dashboard to tell you how the car is running (profitability, productivity, risk), and a windshield to see where you're going (metrics and financial forecasts).

## The Rearview Mirror

Just like a rearview mirror, a Balance Sheet and Operating Statement show you where you've been. Have you piled on debt or piled up cash? Are you making money or burning through it? You need to know.

**BALANCE SHEET:** A Balance Sheet shows what you own (assets) and what you owe (liabilities) at a particular moment in time. It tells you basic things. For example, the difference between your assets and your liabilities is called your net worth. If you and your financial advisors really know how to read a Balance Sheet, you can perform all types of wizardry.

**THE "QUICK RATIO" OR "ACID TEST":** You can divine whether you can meet payroll and other bills if there is a sudden shock to your business and no money comes in. The "quick ratio" or "acid test" compares your "cash" to the bills you have to pay in the next month. For this test, "cash" includes things you can turn into cash very quickly, like short-term government notes. Virtually every banker will run you through this test to determine your financial health. It also matters in times of crisis. When people were afraid to touch their mail after the 2001 anthrax scares, there were plenty of businesses (like mine) that weren't getting any checks from their customers for weeks at a time.

**THE "DEBT RATIO":** You can discover whether you have taken on too much debt in relation to your assets. Your "debt ratio" compares the amount of money you have borrowed to certain assets that you could use to pay those debts. Just like a home owner's borrowing too much money to buy his house and running into trouble when he gets sick or loses his job, too much debt—also called leverage—will jeopardize your business and reduce your ability to get additional loans when you need them.

**THE "AVERAGE COLLECTIONS PERIOD":** You can tell how long it takes your business to turn sales into cash. Your "average collections period" compares your total accounts receivables to your average daily sales. If you have $1 million in accounts receivable—the amount you are owed by customers—and your average daily sales are $30,000, it is taking you a healthy 33 days (1,000,000/30,000 = 33.3) to convert your sales into cash. In tough economic times, your average collections period likely will rise, showing that it is taking your customers longer to pay. That is important to know. As this collection period rises, you need to increase both your collection efforts and the screening of the financial health of prospective customers.

These tests and other tools don't turn lead into gold, but having them is like having a crystal ball.

In Sam's case, he had two big problems with his Balance Sheets. First, he wasn't getting them on time. It was like a doctor looking at an old X-ray. The patient broke a toe months ago, the bone has already healed crooked, and it was too late for a cast. A lotta good that X-ray did.

But even if the Balance Sheets had been timely, they failed to show critical liabilities. Sam's company brokered mortgage loans. He was like a matchmaker for borrowers and lenders. But every time Sam's company brokered a mortgage, he guaranteed the lender that the borrower would make the first payment. That guarantee meant Sam's company was on the hook for the first mortgage payment. So those guarantees should have been recorded as liabilities on the Balance Sheet. Yet his finance folks overlooked them and Sam didn't realize they had risen to tens of millions of dollars. When hundreds of the subprime borrowers failed to pay their new loans—and the lenders came calling for their money—it was like an avalanche of debt snuck up from behind and buried the company.

**OPERATING STATEMENT:** An Operating Statement shows the money coming into your business (revenues) and the money you're paying out (expenses) over various time periods, usually each month and year. When your revenues exceed your expenses you have a profit, and when your expenses are more than your revenues you have a loss. Better still, when you compare your Operating Statement from one time period to another, you can see all kind of important trends. If revenues are up, but your cost of labor isn't, your workers might be more productive than they were before. If your profits have leveled off, you may be facing more competition. With the help of your financial advisors, you can also compare your Operating Statement to similar data from other companies in your industry. You might find that you're paying way too much for certain supplies and should be demanding the same discounts that others get. You could also learn that your rent is too high as a percent of your revenues and you should be cutting better deals or leasing less expensive premises.

You also can't grow your business without the right information. How can you promote your VP of sales if you don't know whether the jobs she's been selling for the last year are profitable? How can you buy new equipment if you don't know whether your debts are already getting out of hand? How can you know whether you must cut costs if you don't know whether you are losing money?

It is also important to focus. Don't collect too much data. Don't prepare too many financial reports. You will not only tie up valuable company resources, but you will also make it harder to study the truly important information.

Doing business today is like changing lanes on the New Jersey Turnpike with an eighteen-wheeler bearing down on you in the left lane. You can't make good decisions if you don't know what's behind you. A Balance Sheet and an Operating Statement—and the insights they provide—are the rearview mirror that will keep you from getting crushed.

But you can't drive a car just by looking in the rearview mirror. You need to know where you're going and that you've got the gas to get there.

## The Dashboard

Most new entrepreneurs have a gut feeling about how their business is running. Heck, most new businesses are so small that you can run from one end of the office or store to the other without getting winded. You know the names of all of your employees. You can even check morale by the looks on their faces. You're also frequently talking to your biggest customers, so you know how they feel. You understand how your business is working. But that doesn't last as you get bigger. You need a dashboard to monitor whether the engine is overheating or the gas is low or you're going too fast.

In every business, there's a variety of measurements that you should be getting from your business dashboard. Here are just a few:

**NET PROFIT MARGIN RATIO:** How profitable are you? Your Net Profit Margin Ratio shows how much money you are making on your sales. Just compare your net profit (profits after all expenses but before you deduct your taxes) to your sales. If you make $800 on every $10,000 of sales, you have an 8 percent Net Profit Margin Ratio, which may be good or bad in comparison to your past performance and the performance of your competitors.

**RETURN ON INVESTMENT RATIO:** What kind of return are you getting on the money that you and others have invested in your business? This investment might be the initial money you put in, the money you added to keep it running, or the money you want an investor to put in to expand the business. The ROI Ratio compares your net profit to your company's net worth. If you have an annual net profit of $100,000 and a net worth of $1 million (net worth equals assets minus liabilities), then you have a 10 percent ROI. You can be sure any investor or purchaser will want to look at this number to see how your company stacks up—profitability-wise—against your competitors.

**INVENTORY TO SALES RATIO:** Is your inventory getting too bloated? The Inventory to Sales Ratio gives you a warning signal about recent swings in your inventory. Compare your inventory balance (usually at the end of month) to your sales for that month. If your inventory is $200,000 and your sales were

$100,000, then you have an Inventory to Sales Ratio of 2:1. This may be fine, unless you have steadily had a 1:1 ratio and the increase shows that sales are plunging—or you're stocking up on too much inventory. You may be tying up valuable cash or running the risk of having to slash prices to unload that excess inventory.

Every business needs different instruments on its dashboard. Sam's should have had a gauge that showed the number of loan defaults in relation to total loans brokered by the company. It would have started flashing red when the subprime borrowers started defaulting on their loans in increasing numbers. Sam could have jumped on the problem and told his loan officers to stop brokering subprime loans. He could have directed his brokers to switch to safer prime loans, where the risk of borrower default was dramatically lower. Sam didn't have a dashboard, so he didn't get the warning signal. His loan officers kept brokering those subprime loans. Those defaults built up like a perfect storm that washed out the road in front of Sam's business.

## The Windshield

The windshield helps you see where you are going. Above all else, this view tells you a lot about future business. But to really make the windshield work for you, you can't get distracted counting cows and playing license plate games. You need to discern the critical data—it's called metrics. Metrics are key indicators that predict future events. In a store, "traffic"—the number of people walking in—is often a good predictor, or metric, for sales.

Almost every business has certain metrics that accurately predict the future:

- If you are in the environmental cleanup business, a good early indicator of future demand is the number of new building permits. Before builders start grading and excavating, they need to test the soil for contamination. If there is an environmental problem, they'll call companies like yours to clean it up. The more projects they start, the more business there will be for your industry.

- Likewise, if you sell anything for the home, like furniture, appliances, or art, the number of new housing starts has historically been a good indicator of future sales.

- If you're an Internet retailer, you may need to monitor gas prices. As the cost of driving to the mall goes up or down, your sales may do the same.

For Sam's business, a critical indicator was home loan interest rates. As the rates went down, refinancing and purchase loans soared. In fact, you could watch the government raise or lower certain interest rates and accurately predict future mortgage volumes.

But the use of metrics isn't just limited to forecasting demand. Metrics can also predict a variety of other factors that will affect the growth of your business. For example, your accounting firm can't grow if you can't recruit new accountants. So you need to have an eye on the enrollment at accounting schools. You also need to determine whether Wall Street is hiring away the cream of each graduating class. The amount of new graduates available for hire will affect your own recruiting efforts, including advertising and on-campus interviewing, and will affect the pay and benefit packages you need to offer to be successful.

Once you have identified the appropriate metrics for your business, develop a system to track and report these indicators. It can be as simple as keeping track of the number of phone calls you get each week from potential new customers inquiring about your services. The important thing is identifying the right metrics and then implementing a system to collect and report the data.

The same rules apply to collecting and reviewing all of the financial data about your business:

1. Determine what information you need to review.

2. Create a system to produce this information.

3. Analyze the information when you get it.

4. Act on this information to keep your business moving forward.

Sam crashed, but he walked away from the wreck and started another business. He's brokering alternate energy now. He also learned some lessons. He's monitoring the price of oil to see how that affects future demand for his products. He gets a weekly report of other metrics, as well as monthly Operating Statements. He's also reviewing a Balance Sheet that identifies all of his obligations. With this information, he's keeping his debt in check and building cash reserves for the things he can't predict. He's back on the road to growing a business.

# 13

## Payday

### *Yours and Your Employees'*

W hy start a company? You're in for grueling hours, strained relationships, tremendous pressure, risk, heartbreak, highs, and
lows. Why do it?

And it's not just about you.

Why would anyone join your company? Whether they get in on the
ground floor or join the team once you're already growing, they're in for
politics, a roller-coaster ride of abundance and scarcity, too little information and too much responsibility, oh—and like you—grueling hours,
strained relationships, tremendous pressure, risk, heartbreak, highs, and
lows. Again, why do it?

Money.

Money is high on the list of reasons, if not squarely on top. You're
all hoping the business will take off like a rocket ship, be the next
Google, and make millionaires of everyone.

For you and those employees who add a lot of value to your company, this is about creating a real Payday. This is not about everyday
salaries-and-benefits. Getting a paycheck and health insurance is important but not enough. A Payday means life-changing money. Ferrari
money. Mansion money. Take-this-job-and-shove-it money. That's a
real Payday, money that fulfills dreams, provides financial security, and
frees you to do what you want.

## The Ground Rules

In whatever form, a Payday is all about rewarding employees with wealth created by the company. There should be winners (those who add value to the company) and there should be losers (those who don't). If you're smart and lucky, everyone will get what they deserve. But it doesn't just happen that way. There are ground rules:

1. Don't commit to giving your employees a "percent" of the company. That is a mistake start-ups make. The founder rounds up half a dozen employees and promises everyone with a college degree 5 percent of the company and everyone else 1 percent. Don't. You'll end up giving away too much. Bill Gates made plenty of his employees into millionaires without promising them a percentage of Microsoft.

2. There is a correct way to offer a Payday. Give your employees the right to earn money based on the success of the company. These rights can take a variety of forms. The most well known is stock options. A stock option provides employees with the right to buy stock at a fixed price. As your employees help grow the value of the company, the price of your stock increases. Using these stock options, your employees can buy stock at low prices and sell it for high prices, pocketing the difference.

   How does this help you avoid giving away too much? Simple. The typical Payday plan allows your company to issue millions of stock options spread among many employees over many years. Other than certain key executives, no individual employee is going to get a meaningful percentage of the company, yet your employees will get enough stock options to make them plenty rich.

3. Do provide a significant Payday for your executive team. Prospective buyers of your company, as well as investors, want to see that your key executives have a big stake in the success of the company—that they bleed company blood. So buyers and investors often insist that you grant some—but not too much—ownership to your executives.

   A good rule of thumb is allocating options on 10 to 15 percent of the company stock to your executive team. Understand, though, that these options are the full stake for all of your executives. Save enough for future additions to the team.

4. Don't throw your stock around like it's a cheap substitute for cash. One start-up I know gave their first Chief Technology Officer 5 percent of the company to make up for a teensy salary. The company looked at their stock like it was "cash helper." Big mistake. The company quickly outgrew his talents. To get rid of him, the company had to buy back the stock for a small fortune—far more than they ever would have had to pay him in salary. Giving stock isn't cheap. When you pay with stock—instead of cash—you're often delaying an even bigger bill.

5. The plan for the owner might not be what you're expecting: the sad fact is, you always get your money last. While you're growing the company, you pay your employees and the bills first. Then you get what's left. When you sell your company, your employees get their Payday and again, you get what's left. Otherwise, there's no special plan for you. Sorry.

6. You need to reward the behavior you want to encourage. If someone doesn't contribute a lot, then he shouldn't get a lot. Maybe all he gets is a nice bonus. Others will be vital to your success and they should be handsomely rewarded. It is

not unusual for a successful Payday to yield payouts ranging from $10,000 to $10 million or more.

## Payday Plans

There is a variety of plans that will create the right Payday for you and your employees. You won't be writing any of them. But you do need to know what questions to ask, what answers sound right, and which plan to sign off on.

First, this is not about throwing cash out of a window onto the sidewalk and spreading the wealth without purpose. This is not confetti and you're not having a parade. No, this is about sparking performance, fueling growth, and incentivizing success.

## Stock Option Plan

The classic Payday plan is a stock option plan. In a typical plan, each year you provide your employees with options to buy company stock.

To get the maximum effect from your plan, you manage volume, valuation, and vesting.

- **Volume** is the number of options you give each employee. Understand these are not party favors. These options are valuable rights that allow your employees to buy company stock at a fixed price. You're giving options because you expect your employees to make the company richer. And you give more if you expect more. For example, you might give your account executive, Sarah, options to buy five thousand shares because you expect her to drive in big accounts and you might only give her assistant, Keith, a fraction of that because he is a beginner.

  With smaller companies, this is a person-by-person analysis. As companies grow, many bestow options based on an employee's salary and/or position. They figure that if they pay someone a substantial six-figure salary or make him a Senior VP, they've already made a judgment that he's adding a lot to the company.

- **Valuation** is all about stock price. An option lets employees buy stock at a fixed price—called the strike price. They get to buy stock at that fixed strike price for a long time, usually ten years, even if the stock price skyrockets. That's how an option motivates. Everyone who gets options is trying to drive up the price of the stock so they can buy at a low strike price and then sell high.

  Where do you set the strike price? Set the strike price at the current value of the stock. If your accountant has just valued the stock at ten dollars per share, the option should let your employees buy company stock at that ten-dollar price. Don't set it lower. You will have enormous tax problems and just be giving money away, not motivating your employees. For example, if the current value is ten dollars per share and your employees get the right to buy it for eight dollars, the first two dollars is just a gift, not a reward. They didn't do anything to earn those two bucks. Likewise, if you set the strike price above the current value, you're discouraging your employees. They don't want to increase the value and not share in it.

- **Vesting** is the amount of time an employee must stay with the company in order to be able to keep and use the options. Remember, this is a plan and you're doing everything for a reason. Here you're trying to reduce turnover and encourage good employees to stick around (I hope you're firing the bad ones). The typical vesting period is three to five years. Once Sarah has stayed with the company for the vesting period, the five thousand options she got are "vested" and absent something extraordinary—like your catching her stealing from the company—her vested option can't be taken away.

If Sarah is at all like the rest of corporate America, once she's vested she will want to know how much her options are worth. If your stock is already being sold publicly, Sarah probably will have a little ticker tape scrolling across her computer screen with a constant update on the stock price. If, like most companies, though, your stock is not publicly traded, there is no ticker tape. Instead your accountant values your stock a few times per year and the head of Human Resources lets everybody know the price.

If the stock has gone up, Sarah could be tempted to buy. The stock might have increased to twenty dollars per share by now and all she has to pay is the ten-dollar strike price. For every one-dollar increase over the strike price, Sarah's original options are worth five thousand dollars more. If she has been with the company for a while and received a lot more stock options, she might be in a position to pocket a substantial six-figure sum.

You may be wondering how Sarah is going to get the money to buy the stock. Usually, she won't need any. If the company is selling their stock to the public, most stock brokerages will feel plenty comfortable lending Sarah enough money for the few days she needs it to pay for the stock—and the low strike price—and then turn around and sell it. If you sell the company, she doesn't need any cash at all. Someone just takes out a calculator and figures out the difference between all of Sarah's strike prices and the final selling price and then gives her a check for the difference. So lack of cash to buy stock is not a really a problem.

Sarah's real problem is, there isn't anyone around to buy the stock from her. Yet. The company isn't selling their stock to the public and can't afford to use their own cash to buy stock back from employees. But all the employees and the owners are in the same boat. They all need a way to cash out. If the company is sold, then everyone with options gets a share of the proceeds. Or the company could start selling its stock to the public, so there would be buyers for everyone's stock. To achieve either of these goals, you have to grow the company and make it very successful. The leaders at your company should be reminding everyone that growth and success are necessary for everyone to achieve their Payday. If you design a stock option plan that links performance to payout and communicate that link to your employees, then stock options can be a powerful motivator and a well-earned reward.

## Money Versus Control

Sarah could decide to buy stock with her options, even though she won't be able to sell the stock yet. This would make her an owner of the company. Ownership gives rights to company money, such as a share of the proceeds from the sale of the business. It also entitles shareholders to dividends if your company ever issues any.

But stock ownership provides other rights that stir up troublesome issues. Though Sarah would own just a small fraction of the company's stock, she would have the right to important company information and the right to attend owner meetings—called shareholder meetings. She could vote on important matters such as electing the Board of Directors and even deciding whether to the sell the company.

Sarah's vote wouldn't be large enough to sway any decisions. Each share of stock usually equals just one vote, and she won't have many shares of stock compared to you and any other founders. Normally, though, you don't want your employees in the boardroom, listening to confidential information and weighing in on ownership decisions. Most owners have enough on their plate without involving their employees in the control of the company. For this reason, a lot of company owners look for alternative Payday plans that will give their employees the economic benefits of stock options, without the extra rights.

## Variations on a Theme

More and more companies are creating Payday plans that strip out all of the rights to control and just provide employees with the right to money if the company is successful. These rights go by a variety of names, but two of the most popular are:

- Stock Appreciation Rights (SARs)

- Unit Appreciation Rights (UARs)

Employees get the same Payday with SARs and UARs as they would from stock options, but they don't crowd the boardroom.

## More Variations

Of course, if your company isn't a corporation, you can't give out options to sell stock—because you don't have any. If you're an LLC, you have membership interests, and if you're a partnership, you have partnership interests. You can do almost anything with these interests that you can with stock. Of course, if you're a sole proprietorship, you don't have any interests at all to give out. But you can still create a plan that rewards employees with bonuses. In each situation, the big issues are similar. How many rights will you provide, how long till they vest, and how much will these rights be worth? A knowledgeable advisor will help you through these issues, as well as the inevitable minefields.

## Minefields

Doughnuts have holes and Payday plans have minefields. It's that simple. It's also true that these minefields exist because you create these Payday plans early on and things change. You don't really know what you're going to need. Also, you got to love 'em, Congress keeps tinkering with tax and compensation laws, planting more mines for the company owner distracted by little things like oh, say, keeping the company running. Here are a few of the mines that are waiting for you and your team:

## Taxes

What tale of woe and warning would be complete without taxes? But taxes are no bit player in this story. Taxes are the lead actor. Many of the Payday explosions come from taxes.

- Your employees could be required to pay taxes well before any Payday, on money they haven't yet received. If the strike price—the price at which they can buy company stock—is set below the current value of the stock at the time they receive their options, taxes are due immediately. That means your employees would have a tax bill now and Payday later. People don't like this. It's also not a big motivator.

- Any Payday plan is subject to immediate taxes if it doesn't satisfy numerous legal requirements. For instance, in 2004 Congress snuck in a law that penalizes "deferred compensation." Congress didn't like the idea that corporate bigwigs were delaying the payout from Payday plans to delay paying taxes. If your plan allows employees to defer their Payday, it may be illegal. Whopping taxes might be due immediately, plus penalties.

- Most investments, including stock, that are held for a year or more are taxed at relatively low capital gains rates. In contrast, salary and any investments held less than a year are taxed at much higher income tax rates. The payout from many Payday plans will be taxed at the higher rates. There's not much you can do about it, but you and your employees should know.

## Employees Versus Independent Contractors

By law, most Payday plans must be made available to all of your full-time employees. Some companies, however, work with a lot of independent contractors. The independent contractors could sue your company, claiming that they should have been treated like employees and allowed to participate in the Payday plan. Sometimes the issue of whether someone is an employee is a close call.

A bunch of independent contractors even sued Microsoft for the right to participate in a Payday plan, arguing that they should be treated like employees. These independent contractors had been paid more per hour than employees but weren't given employee benefits like the Payday plan. They still went to court and won the right to participate in a Payday plan that allowed employees to purchase Microsoft stock at a reduced price.

## Fairness

Once you create a Payday plan, you will have certain legal obligations to be fair to the plan participants. For example, let's say someone is offering you $100 million for your company and the proceeds will be shared with your employees per a Payday plan. You can't reduce the sales price to $90 million and take the $10 million difference in a bogus "consulting" agreement with the purchaser. You are legally required to be fair. You will need to honor both the letter and spirit of your Payday plan.

## Education

Unless you're excited by the prospect of a mob of employees with pitchforks and flaming torches who see you as another Dr. Frankenstein, educate your employees about their Payday plan. It does your business no good if your employees are worrying about how they are going to pay massive tax bills because they didn't understand or know how to handle their Payday. If they are going to have a big tax bill later, let them know now. If they could avoid certain taxes with good advance planning, help them plan.

Also, most Payday plans don't have the punch they could because employees don't understand them. Teach them. Remind them. Everybody benefits.

There are many reasons to start your own company or go to work for someone else's. For the owner, it may be a need to be your own boss or a desire to prove you're successful. For employees, it may the vision of the company, its culture or values, or an opportunity to achieve. Whatever these other reasons, the right plan can reward all of the long hours, hard work, and risk with a real Payday.

# 14

## Risk Management and Compliance

*Avoiding Bad Stuff*

H ow bad could it be?" asked Peter. He and his brother, Ethan, were partners in a dry-cleaning business. They were sitting across the desk from me and began what I generously call their side of the story.

"See, we get the dry-cleaning chemical in these containers—," Peter started.

"—and we load it into the dry-cleaning machine," Ethan finished. "But sometimes we spill it."

"Then we take this squeegee broom and push the spill into the sewer drain in the floor. Presto. Gone. What's the big deal?"

Strangely, they both looked satisfied, like there was a thought bubble over their heads that said: "Problem solved!"

"Are you guys crazy? That chemical is toxic!" I exclaimed.

"Well, sure, there's a lot of warnings and fine print on the container. But hey, we live in a dangerous world," said Peter.

And then, in unison, like it was a family motto, they both said, "You can't be afraid of everything."

Well, there are some things you should be afraid of. Like bankruptcy and prison.

Some people starting a business have a narrow view of success. They obsess about ringing up sales, getting contracts, and bringing home the bacon. In their blind haste to make money, they ignore risks that could kill their business. And in their zeal to succeed, they violate laws and put their business—and freedom—in jeopardy.

Peter and Ethan treated the rules like they were for other people. But now the brothers had really screwed up. It was all there in the lawsuit on my desk. They had unleashed a lethal plume of cancer-causing chemicals on a nearby neighborhood. The solvent that they pushed down the drain leaked through cracks in the sewer line. It could threaten the drinking water of many families in a nearby neighborhood who were still using wells.

I read Peter and Ethan the riot act: "You've endangered people's health. The cleanup could cost millions. You could lose your business and much more."

Finally humbled and afraid, they came clean about another transgression. They admitted that they had two sets of cash registers. One register "Uncle Sam" knew about, and the other he didn't. They shut down Uncle Sam's register at 6:00 P.M. and used the tax-free register during the evening rush. To quote our fearless duo, "We wouldn't even get out of bed and go to work in the morning if it wasn't for that second cash register."

These guys were reckless. They blew off the rules and the risks for years and it finally blew up in their faces. All of that was going to stop.

You don't make money in bankruptcy and you can't spend it in prison. Risk matters. The law matters. They finally understood that.

"If you just help us out of this," they pleaded, "we swear we'll be good."

## Risk

Risk is the potential for harm. We face it every day. When we step off the curb to cross the street, we risk getting run over.

In business, risk is every threat your company faces. If your business is farming, you face the risk that your crops will freeze or flood or that prices will collapse for your products or that fuel will cost so much it won't make sense to harvest your crops.

If you have a construction company, you run the risk that your estimator will underbid the job or your supervisors won't manage the crews efficiently or lumber, drywall, and steel prices will skyrocket or become scarce.

These may not be your risks, but none of us are immune. We all face the risk that we won't find enough qualified employees or a big competitor will enter our market and try to wrestle away our clients with overwhelming resources or our customers' needs will change and our sales will plummet. As a nation of businesses, we risk fire and blizzards, oversupply and shortages, bubbles and crashes, inflation and deflation, free trade and trade sanctions.

Risk is everywhere.

## The Law

Just like risk, every business runs a gauntlet of laws. Take that same construction company. It must hire legal employees per the I-9 requirements and keep their workers safe under OSHA regulations and build apartments and hotels in compliance with FHA and ADA laws and invoice government customers per FAR and DFAS, all the while making sure they don't violate the Patriot Act, the Fair Labor Standards Act, the Equal Opportunity Act, and the We-Made-It-Up-Just-to-Screw-with-You Act.

The Law is everywhere.

## Managing Risk and Complying with the Law

Everyone in business is always thinking about the upside. But you need to think about what might go wrong and how to prevent the downside. It's like a colonoscopy for your business—no fun, but necessary.

You can't avoid risks and legal requirements. The key is to manage those risks and comply with the law. The first demands judgment and the second requires knowledge.

You need the right judgment to understand, evaluate, and respond to the risks you face. You need to know the laws that apply to your business and then comply.

## Risk Management

With risk, you are dealing with varying chances that different bad things will happen. You might have a one-in-ten-thousand chance of being hit by a blackout. You could have a one-in-a-hundred chance that your customers won't pay on time and you will run out of cash. You may have a one-in-ten chance that you will lose your biggest customer to a competitor offering a better deal. Determine what risks you face, measure their importance to your business, and decide how to protect against each one. If you're smart, you'll evaluate these risks properly and allocate the most resources to the greatest threats. As these risks change, you need to rebalance everything. That takes a lot of judgment.

One client I had was hauling dirt in a hundred dump trucks all over the Mid-Atlantic. During our risk review, they admitted they only had $1 million of insurance coverage—total—for all of those trucks. We stopped the meeting right then, while I had them call their insurance broker and increase the coverage to $10 million. The extra coverage wasn't a big expense for them; they just hadn't thought about the potential risk. A few months later, one of their trucks was in a horrible accident. People were badly hurt. It was a tragedy for all involved. But the increased insurance paid for their medical bills and the care they would need for the rest of their lives—and kept the company out of bankruptcy.

Let's break this one down:

**HIGH-PROBABILITY RISK:** Over a few years, it was inevitable one of their trucks would get in an accident. Call it 100 percent chance.

**GREAT HARM:** These were big trucks carrying heaving loads. Think elephant in a china shop. Call it a big loss.

So we had a 100 percent certainty of a horrible outcome. The only question was what to do about it.

**THE RISK WAS MANAGEABLE:** We bought more insurance at affordable rates. We also trained our drivers, checked their driving records, and maintained the trucks.

That's managing risk.

Early on, most entrepreneurs have a gut instinct for the risks they face and the way to address them. As you grow, here's how you manage risk:

1. *Assess Risks.* At least once per year, assess the risks to your company. Your outside advisors, especially your insurance consultant, can give you a good idea of what threats lurk. These advisors usually work with a lot of other companies and can share horror stories. You may not be immune.

2. *Assign Probabilities.* You can only make an educated guess, but try to determine the odds of each thing that could go wrong.

3. *Predict the Harm.* How bad will it be? Will you be cutting bonuses or cutting staff?

4. *Respond.* Address the risks—worst first. You may need any number of things, such as insurance, training, or cash reserves.

5. *Don't Go to Sleep.* Risks change over time. Don't stop evaluating and responding.

## Complying with the Law—It's Simple

Don't break the law. You don't want to manage your business by indictment.

Don't break the law out of ignorance. Like they say on every cop show, ignorance of the law is no excuse.

Know the laws that apply to your business. For example, if you're exporting technology, you need to know there are laws that regulate what you're allowed to export. Loral Space and Communications, Ltd., sold satellites. In the 1990s, they assisted the Chinese government after two rocket launches failed. Loral faced severe penalties because this assistance allegedly violated export control laws. They didn't admit anything, but they ended up paying a $14 million fine, spent another $6 million to prevent future problems, and agreed to hire a Corporate Compliance Officer.

You can't win if you don't know the rules. Knowing the law gives you the opportunity to work the system—legally. For example, you may be trying to shelter income from taxes. If you get an accountant's written opinion that the shelter is legal, you can avoid penalties even if the IRS says your shelter is bogus. You can be sure the IRS is never going to give you that tip. But by knowing the law, you save yourself a pile of money. As a buddy of mine says about attorneys, "You guys always win. You have the 'rule book.' "

Then there are shades of gray. One businessman wanted to give paid leave to his longtime assistant for her pregnancy. But he didn't give paid leave to other employees, like the guys in the warehouse who hurt their backs lifting furniture. The problem was that if he only gave her paid time off, then it might be considered illegal discrimination. Still, he was determined to do something special for her. She had been with him for two decades, knocking herself out to make him look good. Instead of giving her paid leave, he got creative and gave her a big bonus for all her years of outstanding service. Coincidentally, this bonus covered the pay she missed while she was out on unpaid leave. It's not all black and white.

But most of the time, all you can and should do is comply—even if that forces you to change your business. It's not really a business if you're breaking the law—think Napster. They weren't technically "stealing," but they certainly weren't complying with the law.

So if the law is a jungle, here is the machete:

**SURVEY:** Know what's out there. Scan the universe of laws that surrounds your business. It sounds like a lot. But if you're going to build a business of any value, if you're really going to sell it for a fortune, it can't be breaking the law.

**AUDIT:** Determine what you need to do to comply. Some requirements are going to be clear-cut. Others are in a "gray area" because some laws are badly written or vague or don't make sense. Get the right advice and determine what applies.

**PLAN:** Create a compliance program.

**TEST:** Monitor your compliance.

Even a profitable business can be torpedoed if you don't manage risks or comply with the law. Ask the folks at WorldCom, Enron, Fannie Mae, Freddie Mac, AIG, Lehman Brothers, Wachovia, WaMu, Circuit City, National City. The list goes on. Whether it's risks or laws, you've got to protect your business.

## On the Other Hand . . .

You may be completely committed to risk management and the law when you leave your attorney's office or your annual compliance meeting. But like an ex-smoker in a bar, you may slip into old bad habits or feel peer pressure to cheat.

Why do so many businesses run afoul of the law? Why do colossal companies ignore gigantic risks? What's going on with them that also could trip you up? They have issues.

## The Herd Mentality

Sometimes we are not that different from a bunch of five-year-olds mimicking one another's bad behavior. If all your friends are buying credit swaps that are poorly collateralized, then why not you? Just because everyone else is doing it doesn't make it right. Think for yourself.

## The Slippery Slope

A lot of felony convictions started with little things, like fudging expense reports or inflating your résumé. Once you crack open the door, you're tempted to walk right in. Keep it shut.

## "I'll Never Get Caught"

Just because you're driving on an empty highway doesn't make it legal to speed. "No one will ever catch me" is not the same as "it's legal." Besides, ex-spouses and ex-employees can blow the whistle, an audit can nail you, a curious bank teller can call the Feds, or an aggressive attorney general can make you his cause. That should keep you up at night.

It doesn't matter if everyone else is doing it. It doesn't make a difference if you started small. It doesn't help if you think you'll never get caught. At best you're playing Russian roulette with your business, and at worst you lose everything.

Peter and Ethan, our intrepid dry cleaners, didn't go to prison. They didn't even lose their houses. Whoever said this was a story about justice? But cleaning that polluted soil took every penny they had—including all the money that went into their tax-free cash register.

I made them get rid of that second cash register. I also tried hard but couldn't convince them to pay their back taxes. They thought they paid enough already when they cleaned up their mess. So that IRS risk is still hanging over their heads.

As with a lot of businesses, managing risk and complying with the law didn't come easily. It took the scare of their lives to get them to change, and even then they didn't go back and right all wrongs. But they swear their cheating days are over. As they like to remind me, "We're the only dry cleaners around who are really clean."

# 15

## Implementation

### *Better to Implement a Good Plan Than Seek a Perfect One*

Nothing is perfect.

Name one perfect, flawless thing. Even the most valuable diamonds in the world have imperfections—so many, they grade the flaws. If you're determined to make something perfect, then you'll never succeed.

The same goes for business. You're only hurting your company if you're counting on perfection. If you won't act until you have the perfect plan, then plan on waiting.

Some businesses don't get it. All that studying and analysis and still we get bombs like the Edsel, New Coke, and all of the later *Star Wars* movies. Then there's "endless meeting land." We've all sat in those marathons, working on the perfect plan, estimating market share, plotting strategy, parsing key assumptions, and, my personal favorite, requesting further analysis.

What do we have here? They call it planning, but it's just a bunch of people watching slides, shuffling paper, and listening to the sound of their own voices. It's activity but not progress—like a hamster running on a wheel. Planning is essential, but not when it paralyzes your business. You need structure and rules for effective planning—and then you need to get moving.

## Planning Pointers

**START WITH THE END:** No planning process should begin without a clear understanding of your goals.

**TO ENSURE YOUR PLANNING MEETINGS ARE PRODUCTIVE, SET AN AGENDA AND A TIME LIMIT FOR EVERY MEETING:** Each meeting should finish with a "to do" list.

**DEMAND ACCOUNTABILITY:** Everyone needs to finish their homework and present it at the next meeting. One of the best reasons for meeting is that it forces people to get their work done. They don't want to show up empty-handed.

## The Proof Is in the Putting—Putting Your Plan to the Test

A plan—even a "great" one—is still just a bunch of words and charts. You can assume customer demand and predict sales, but the best plan is about as accurate as a weather prediction. Whether you're planning a single product or an entire business, you don't really know what works until you test it with reality. You'll learn more from trying out your plan than from formulating it.

One client, Johnny, was convinced that the next big business would be fixing computers for home-based businesses and tech-friendly families. He surveyed consumers, studied household incomes, and researched the labor pool. It all worked—on paper.

But that didn't mean Johnny was going to make any money in the real world. So he decided to let reality be the judge. His first customer was a woman with a dead computer. He warned her that the repairs could wipe out the memory. She assured him that she had backed up everything. He fixed the computer, but within moments she starting shrieking, "My photos are gone! I didn't think you meant them." She refused to pay and threatened to sue. It only got worse. Customers didn't show up for appointments, bounced checks, and haggled over prices.

The test shocked Johnny. It also saved him a bundle. The world wasn't ready for his business. Implementing your plan doesn't mean it will succeed. But that is the best way to find out.

Still, don't just dive in with no plan—that's the "Ready-Fire-Aim" method. Action, just for the sake of action, is too risky. It's like jumping out of a plane without checking to see if your parachute works. Instead, balance planning and implementation. Once you've thought it through and formulated a good plan, jump.

Who knows what will happen? We're always surprised. It's never what you think it's going to be.

## Plans Give You Predictions; Implementation Gives You Answers

Even successful companies freeze up when it comes to implementing new plans. I was sitting in a board meeting for an established company whose sales were about to fall off a cliff. A new law was going to kill their biggest-selling product.

They had seen the change coming and had been working on new products. But they kept revising their plan over and over and over again. Outside advisors posed far-fetched hypotheticals. Defensive department heads struggled to respond to these crazy scenarios. The President demanded sales estimates and the CFO—who was pale and looked like he would faint at any moment—stuttered out cautious assurances. This was the umpteenth meeting to review the plan, and each time someone raised an objection they went back to the drawing board.

Their past success paralyzed them. They were afraid to launch the new plan until they were positive it would perform as well as the old one. But they were going to run out of money and fail if they didn't get started right away. "You're never going to know if the new plan will work," I urged, "until you try." Everyone turned around and looked at me like they were seeing indoor plumbing for the first time.

After some muttering and hesitation, they agreed it was time to launch the new plan. Sure, there were problems, but not what they predicted. Ultimately they were successful, but only by starting did they discover the real challenges.

Here's the key if you're like these folks and afraid to implement: Just start. Don't worry about success. Test your concept and gather data. Then study the results and use them to refine your plan. For many, this psychological trick—treating your plan like an experiment—helps overcome the fear of failure.

Once you implement, it's all right in front of you—answers, not predictions. Some ideas will fall flat on their faces. Some of your worst fears may evaporate. There may be tremendous demand for your new product. Or your new service may be impossible to produce at an affordable price. But then again, you may have just discovered a new drug so fantastically successful that it is unethical to keep giving some people placebos during clinical trials. Rather than endlessly planning, launch your concept.

You're never going to find success in a plan. A plan on a drawing board is a theory—perhaps even a great idea. But only a plan in action can work. That's why it's better to implement a good plan than seek a perfect one.

# 16

# Contracts

*Because a Handshake Won't Do*

I was sworn in as an attorney on December 19, 1985, and Nick became my first and only client a day later. I was a regular at his sub shop, where he made a killer chicken with pesto on a crispy Italian roll. He also owned a bunch of storefronts in a seedy part of town that he rented out to small merchants. Nick found himself haggling endlessly with tenants when he should have been making sandwiches. I told him as much. So he came down to my office. "I'm tired of all the negotiating. All that back-and-forth, it's too much," he said as he pounded his fist on my desk. "Protect me. But make the lease something the tenants will sign. No negotiations!" He handed me a lease the size of a book, and a bag of sandwiches as a down payment on my fee, before he walked out of my office.

The lease was way too tough. First I got rid of all the crazy penalties and one-sided provisions. Nick didn't even know they were there, much less want to enforce them. But the lease still invited negotiations. It was so massive it forced small businesspeople to take it to a lawyer. The margins were wide, as on a notepad for revisions. The economic terms of the deal were spread throughout, forcing even the laziest person to study the whole document.

It was makeover time. I pushed the margins out to the edges of the paper so there would be no room for comments. Of course, someone could write changes on a separate piece of paper, but most wouldn't bother. Then I took the business terms that were spread throughout the lease and put them on the first page. Once most people got to those, they would stop reading. I also shrunk the font and put the text on both sides of long paper. That took the lease down to five sheets from forty. Then I formatted it to look like a preprinted rental car lease. Who negotiates those?

Nick came back the next day. He liked my handiwork. "Good, but more," he grunted. He stood over my shoulder while I changed the name of the document from "Lease" to "Standard Lease." Then at the bottom of each page I added "Form No. 2235," so tenants would think Nick got the lease from a dime store. That was the first time I saw him smile. "That's it. That's it," he said, and looked at me like he had found a husband for his only daughter.

Nick was thrilled with the results. Before, he had a bad contract that no one would sign without a struggle. Now the tenants checked the rent on the first page, skimmed through the rest, then flipped to the last page and signed. The contract was shorter, fairer, and friendlier to the tenants. Nick got what he wanted—a good contract that flew under the radar instead of sticking out like a sore thumb.

No more negotiating for Nick. Free sandwiches for me.

As Nick learned, you don't need to live with a bad contract. Don't treat it lightly—whether your side is drafting the agreement or you're responding to someone else's document. If it's important enough to have a contract, then it's important enough to have a good one. But many people don't. They think it's too expensive or too much trouble to get a good contract. Or they don't even realize what they're doing. They sign contracts like stars sign autographs. They wouldn't know a good contract if you shoved one in their face.

## What Is a Good Contract?

We enter into contracts every day. Every time we click on the terms of services of a Web site, we enter into an extensive contract. We don't read them, but we're certainly signing them electronically. We become bound by contracts everywhere, when we buy a lift ticket at a ski resort or drop off our laundry at the cleaner or even take our car to the wash (when you read the sign with the rules—or ignore it—and drive through). Face it: you get more contracts than sex.

So how about some good ones? Contracts, that is.

A good contract does two things. It commits everything important to writing, which keeps you out of court most of the time. And if you have to go to court, it helps you win. Bottom line: it captures your deal and protects you. How does this happen?

One side starts with a term sheet—their wish list. The other side hacks that up with their obnoxious requests. Everyone gets realistic—eventually—and the term sheet starts to resemble something both sides can live with. People hear what they want to, so all of this has to be in writing. It forces people to be clear and lets each side know what they're really getting.

Then somebody drafts the contract to include the agreed-upon terms and flesh out the details. You'll still have some back-and-forth but a lot less disagreement when the agreement matches the term sheet. This process of drawing out the parties' expectations and summarizing the major terms speeds contract preparation and reduces disputes.

Still, people being what they are, you need to be prepared for a fight in the future. If you and the other side don't agree later, the contract has to establish how you resolve that dispute. Are you going to court? Are you arbitrating? Does the loser pay the winner's legal fees? What are your remedies? Can you terminate the agreement if the other side breaches? Are you reimbursed if you need to hire someone else to finish the contract? There are dozens of important questions that must be answered to make sure you are protected.

If you're not an attorney, how do you know you have a good contract? The simple fact is that most people—including a lot of lawyers—don't know good legal work. Picking good legal work is a little bit like picking a good surgeon. It's hard. ("He seems like a nice guy. I guess he won't sever any of the arteries that go to the important stuff.") It takes a *good* lawyer to know good legal work. So the best answer is to get a good lawyer to read the contract—whether your lawyer wrote it or someone else did. I know, big help I am. Now you're thinking you have to find two good lawyers, one to pick the other. Sorry.

But if you're not a legal expert, you can still audit a contract to see if it's good:

- Make sure the contract contains all of the key terms of the deal.

- Confirm people are willing to sign it. It shouldn't be so one-sided no one will agree to it.

- Check for redundancy. The contract should say it once, clearly, and not in multiple overlapping provisions. Unnecessary repetition is a sign of a bad contract. The writer is potentially leaving you with conflicting provisions that each side can use in a fight.

- Watch for excess. Nothing slows down a deal like an over-the-top contract that strangles the other side. There shouldn't be massive penalties for minor infractions, especially if they are unenforceable.

- Inspect for irrelevancy. For example, if your deal has nothing to do with hazardous materials, then you don't need three pages of hazmat definitions and restrictions. Don't let someone else's master form become your contract if it doesn't fit.

- Make sure that your contract addresses the what-ifs. What if the other side breaches? What if the other side goes bankrupt? What if the price of some key material goes up? What if you can't deliver your end of the bargain? You know what could go wrong, so make sure the contract does, too.

## ~~Good~~ Great Contracts

Usually, a good contract is all you need. But a great contract can be like Miracle-Gro for the growth and sale of your company. When you have the opportunity, here's how you go for the gold:

**"THE HOMETOWN ROAST":** Just like in sports, you get an edge from the home field advantage. If you're doing business across the country, you want a contract that says that all litigation must take place in your home state. Often the judge and jury give the home team the benefit of the doubt. Sometimes they do more—the traveling team is frequently flame broiled by the locals. The disadvantage to the other side is so notorious that lawyers have nicknamed it "the hometown roast."

**MOST FAVORED NATION CLAUSE:** This one is a peach. You're telling the other side they can't offer anyone else a better deal. If they want to give someone else a better agreement, they have to come back and sweeten your contract, so that it stays better than everyone else's. You only get this clause with a lot of bargaining power—the other side really needs your business (or can't read).

**EXTENSION AND EXPANSION:** If you already have a good deal, get more. For example, you might have a five-year agreement to buy bottled water at a fixed price from a famous spring. Demand and sales could soar. Get an option to extend the agreement for five more years. Also get the right to buy more bottled water over time. These extension and expansion rights could be extremely valuable to you and anyone who wants to buy your business.

**TERMINATION FOR CONVENIENCE:** Called a T for C, this right allows you to terminate the contract for any reason—or no reason at all—and just pay the other side for the work they've done. It adds value by allowing you to cut your losses. Say demand for office space plunges. A developer with this right could terminate a construction contract to avoid spending more to finish a building that won't lease.

**EXCLUSIVITY:** Who wouldn't want a monopoly, especially when it means yours is the only business that can sell beer in the stadium? Exclusivity locks out the competition. You're the only one who can sell your products in a given market, allowing you to increase prices and your sales.

## Praying over Commas

There is a breed of businesspeople that doesn't believe contracts are important. I've worked with them for decades. I call them pay-you-later guys. They're smart and hardworking and know their business. I admire them. But they have a weakness. They won't pay an ounce for prevention, but they get stuck paying a ton for cures. All someone has to do to rob them blind is hand them a contract. They check the math but don't read the rest of the agreement. They won't have their attorney review or negotiate the contract—they think the whole process is a ruse to whip up fees. They have faith their friendship with the other side will overcome any disputes. They sign, happy in the knowledge that "it's all boilerplate, anyways."

Then something bad happens. Their new software product crashes. Their pipeline breaks and floods downtown. Their vaccine is late and misses the window for flu season. People are injured. Money is lost. Lawsuits fly. Armageddon approaches. Suddenly the contract they neglected becomes a sacred document. They pore over that agreement like Talmudic scholars studying an ancient scroll. Guys who haven't read anything but *Golf Digest* for thirty years are studying clauses and pointing out irrelevant minutiae that they claim exonerates them—relationships be damned!

"He signed with red ink. That can't be legal! Right?"

"He dated the contract the day after we actually signed it. So, no deal. Right?"

"So we're sitting there signing the thing and he never blinks. I'm not even sure he's human. I'm good. Right?"

I call it praying over commas. They're praying some little detail or wacky theory is going to rescue them. It's not. What they're ignoring is the fact that the other side paid a lot of money to prepare a contract that's enforceable. Of course, every now and then you can turn chicken poop into chicken salad. Sometimes the other side will fumble the ball on the one-yard line. But don't count on it.

Instead of wishful thinking, try these instead:

- Read the contract. Before you sign it. All the way through to the end. It sounds simple, but you would be shocked how many people don't. I know it's boring and tedious. Personally, I wouldn't do it if I wasn't getting paid to. But a famous NFL player, LaVar Arrington, didn't get a $6.5 million bonus that he claimed was supposed to be in his contract. His agent admitted to being in a rush and not reading the final draft of the agreement. The agent was punished by the NFL, but that didn't put any money in LaVar's pocket.

- Pay attention to definitions. In contracts, millions of dollars can turn on the meaning of a word. Sometimes much more. After 9-11, there were enormous court battles over whether the New York terrorist attacks were one "occurrence" or two. Billions of dollars hung in the balance. If each plane crash was a separate occurrence, the owner of the World Trade Center would get twice as much money from the insurance companies.

- Comply with the law. The law regulates all kinds of contracts, especially those with consumers. Contracts for everything from gym memberships, to houses, to door-to-door sales have special requirements. When you don't comply, you can be fined and often the consumer can get out of the agreement. When the real estate market plunged, thousands of would-be home buyers tore up their purchase agreements and got their deposits back because the seller overlooked things like handing the purchaser a two-inch stack of home owners' association documents. You've got to know what the law requires and then do it—so there is no back door out of your agreements.

- Be prepared. You should always have your own form contracts for regular parts of your business. Don't wait until you need the agreement for a particular deal or you may get stuck using the other side's form because you're moving fast. If you're using the other side's agreement, you may face a one-sided contract that hurts you or requires massive revisions.

- Draft, baby, draft. You're more likely to get what you want if you prepare the first draft of the agreement. Your changes to someone else's agreement tend to make you look difficult, especially if you want a lot of them. Better to write it your way the first time. If you can't, you're often forced to pick your battles.

- Don't go overboard. Some contracts are like an intelligence test. If the other side signs it, they fail. If you insist on an extremely tough contract, count on doing business with idiots.

- Keep it as short as you can.

Good contracts pay. Bad contracts will cost you.

# 17

## Marketing

*It's Not Who You Are.*

*It's Who They Think You Are.*

Sacha would have been a witch doctor in another time or place. She was always cooking up some concoction for burns or dry skin or upset stomachs. When other people were busy surfing the Net or watching television, she had her nose burrowed in dusty old books, researching centuries-old folk remedies. Sacha even looked the part—not Goth, more granola—with wiry gray hair, no makeup, and knitted poncho sweaters. She looked like some throwback from the eighteenth-century English countryside. You half-expected to find sheep grazing in the backyard of her town house. But oh, did she have fans.

She cured people's ills. They got her potions as gifts and loved the stuff. People got so hooked they begged her to start selling these creations. After much prodding, she finally began peddling small batches, even to a few strangers who heard of her powers by word of mouth.

But it was just a hobby. Though she dreamed about making a business of it, she was afraid to plunge into a venture that she feared would fail—and with good reason. Poor Sacha lost money on every sale. So she kept her day job proofreading reports at the Pentagon. She hated it but did it for her parents and the steady paycheck.

For my fortieth birthday, Sacha gave me her "Special Super Smooth" lotion for dry skin. I had long ago given up on the sandpaper skin on my heels, but Sacha urged me to give it a try. After three days my heels were as soft as a baby's butt. I was sold. Better still, I wanted to help her realize her dream.

But how to turn Sacha's hobby into a business?

It wasn't just that her ingredients were secret. So were her products. She didn't have a brochure, a Web site, or even business cards. All she had was handwritten recipes. Her idea of viral marketing was selling immune-boosting tea to people with the flu.

Plenty of people were eager to pay for her potions—she just needed to get her message out. But she simply didn't get the concept of marketing. Her parents grew up in the First Great Depression and had passed on a kind of thriftiness that steered clear of any flashiness. She was a coupon clipper, not a Juicy Couture lady. The few lotions she sold were plopped into old mayonnaise jars and squirt bottles. She handwrote the labels on masking tape with a butcher's grease pen. She was all substance and no style.

## Style Points

Marketing could change that. I explained to Sacha that marketing is all about promoting your product and there were a number of ways she could do that:

**BRANDING:** Historically, a brand was a symbol burned onto animals with a searing-hot iron to show who owned the beasts. Now it's both a logo that symbolizes a product or business and a summary of what your company and/or product is all about. Usually it's visual—Nike's "swoosh" is a world-famous brand about athletes in motion. But often sound, smell, and touch become brands. Intel's "Intel Inside" sound and NBC's chimes each brand their products. Johnson & Johnson's clean, sweet smells brand their baby products. And who hasn't squeezed the

Charmin and understood that a brand can be about touch? Ultimately, a brand conveys some unique, essential, and lasting truth about your product or business.

**ADVERTISING:** This is everything from craigslist, to radio and TV commercials, to billboards, to Valpak coupons, to Internet banners. You can pay to get your ads on the sides of trucks and hot-air balloons, fly messages over crowded beaches, and place your products in movies.

**PUBLIC RELATIONS:** More creativity and energy are required to get the media to run stories that put your business or product in a favorable light. A whole industry has arisen to issue press releases about you, get a video crew out to your office for an interview, and publish your articles. Often called earned media, this publicity gives your message even more credibility than advertising because you're not supposed to be able to buy it. In reality, you pay indirectly because you hire talented and con-nected people, often former media personnel, to pitch your story.

There's a lot more to marketing. For better or worse, marketing is also the way you answer the phone, the way you dress, and the décor of your office or store. Everything you do affects how customers view your business. The dying plant in the doctor's office says to patients "That could be me." Add in a few ten-year-old *Family Circle* magazines and faded old *Highlights* and the only thing keeping you in that wait-ing room is a low deductible.

Substance matters. Skill is critical. But most people don't know whether a doctor is a good surgeon or a car is well made or a pill will cure their ills. People judge by appearances. My clients could be read-ing the most brilliant document I've ever drafted, but if there is a typo on page 49, the aura is gone. Presentation is paramount.

This is unfortunate for talented wallflowers but terrific for good marketers.

## The Sacha Project

So there I was in my first marketing meeting with a shrinking violet. Sacha knew slippery elm bark would sooth a sore throat, echinacea could rev up your immune system, and raw honey was a great salve for burns. But she didn't know not to tuck her shirt into her underwear. We had to make that work for us. Branding in particular and marketing in general are all about selling a better you. But it's still you. You can't fake it, certainly not forever. Don't try.

Sacha had that Wiccan-Wonder-bearing-gifts-from-Mother-Earth thing going on. So we created a logo of a witch standing over a cauldron with the brand name "Sacha's Brew". This branding would go on all of her products and marketing.

We revolutionized her packaging—switching from used mayo jars to new mayo jars. But these had cauldron-shaped brown paper labels— bearing the logo and brand name—and a hemp string tied around every jar. Very granola—but with a touch of good witch Glinda.

Next we tackled her Web site, knowing how much people search and shop on the Internet. In today's world, if you don't have a Web site, it's like having a store without an address or front door. She loaded up great pictures of each product with fables describing the historical origin of each product, in just the right witchy font. Of course, her Web site also had all of the modern conveniences, from online ordering, to PayPal payment, to FedEx deliveries. You could sign up for e-mails about future product offerings, view her "Sacha Says" blog, or join an online discussion about health-care issues.

With her brand in place, her products newly packaged, and the electronic storefront open, we saved precious advertising dollars and set out to earn some media. Our PR friend, working at a drastic discount (a lifetime supply of Sacha's Shingles-free Supreme!), whipped up press releases that got the ball rolling. In a concession to our 24/7 on-the-go no-sleep world, we ran with a story about ancient remedies for modern times. Sacha's witch hazel lotion would remove those bags under your eyes, her valerian-root tea would help you sleep, and her bilberry jam would help your blurry vision. But what really hooked the local Fox channel was her Chinese herbal remedy that vied with Viagra for spicing up the boudoir. It didn't hurt that our PR guy used to be a reporter at the station and knew all of the producers in town. Soon Sacha was all over the news.

She rode that wave. Sacha uploaded her TV spots to YouTube, created a Facebook group, and started tweeting updates on Twitter. She even became a regular guest on a few news programs, touting the latest volcanic-mud acne zapper and all-natural willow-bark painkiller. Sales soared. With the increased demand, Sacha finally made a critical leap—she was able to buy her raw ingredients and packaging in bulk. That drove costs way down and pushed her into profitability. Now she actually made money on each sale. Abracadabra and poof: Sacha turned her hobby into a business.

Sacha discovered that people judge things based on appearances. She didn't like it. But she learned to work it.

Sacha's was no overnight success. She honed her craft—in obscurity. There was something important missing. Once she understood that there's a difference between having a great product and selling it, she committed the time and money to publicizing her message. She even moved in with parents, rented out her town house, and used her reliable government paycheck to fund the limelight. In time, she was able to quit her day job and turn her passion into a profitable business. The potions were powerful, but the marketing was the real magic.

# 18

## Government Relations

*Making Friends in High Places*

M ost subpoenas come in thick envelopes. Ours certainly did.
It sat there on the conference table waiting to be opened.
We all had an inkling of what was inside, and we would have just as
soon gone home for the day and let someone else deal with it.

My client was a highly regulated financial services company. It's an
industry in a field full of land mines. One consumer complaint could
trigger a multiyear Attorney General investigation or a U.S. Senate
hearing. One consumer complaint could trigger a class action lawsuit,
cost a fortune in legal fees, and bury you in an avalanche of adverse
publicity.

And guess what? All of that bad stuff exploded from that envelope
and a couple of others just like it that we received over the next few
weeks.

As we stared at that first envelope, one thought hung over the
room. Howie, the CEO, looked at me and asked, "Is it too late to start
that government relations program that you've been noodging me
about for years?"

Yes. It was too late.

The advice that I had been giving Howie about starting a government relations program is the same table pounding that I had been
doing for my clients for years. Invest in the process. Get to know the
power players. Contribute. Host a fund-raiser and attend a bunch of

others. Network. Get others to give. Hire a lobbyist. Get out the vote. In short, make friends in high places.

Why do it? Because anybody can get in trouble. Because there are thousands of laws and regulations and too many "gray" areas. Because you and your colleagues sometimes make stupid mistakes. Because there are government paper pushers who have all the time in the world to torture you with endless investigations. Because, as Howie discovered, one consumer complaint can lead to an envelope full of troubles.

The government asked Howie's company for hundreds of thousands of documents that the investigators never intended to read yet kept demanding. Top executives were tied up answering questions and distracted from their business plan. Growth went out the door, along with some good employees. Business decreased and it was harder to hire new employees. Suitors previously interested in investing in or even buying the company shied away and took a "wait and see" approach. The media coverage didn't help, either.

The fate of your company may hinge on an effective government relations program. Think of it as insurance. And no one's selling policies as the hurricane rolls in. Or think of it like fire extinguishers and parachutes. It's there just in case. In a crisis, you need the power players to return your calls, you need to be able to meet with the right people, and you need a fair hearing of your concerns. The power players don't run when you're in trouble; they actually stop and help—although there are no guarantees. And when you're just trying to get a law passed or quash someone else's, a good program may actually sway a vote or two—which could make all the difference.

Here's how you do it.

**STEP ONE:** Identify the politicians, rule makers, and regulators who affect your business. Who passes the laws and regulations? Is it the local, state, or national legislature or some governmental agency? Who polices your industry? Is it the state's attorney in your county, the Attorney General for your state, or the Justice Department in D.C.?

**STEP TWO:** Establish a plan and budget for building relationships with these people.

**STEP THREE:** Get to work. This may mean putting a lobbyist or three on retainer. You may want to set up a political action committee to fund contributions to politicians. Contribute, hold fund-raisers, and encourage others to do so. Meet with the key delegates, representatives, and committee chairs who affect your industry. Invite them to see your business and get to know you better. Learn about their view of your industry. Ask them how you might be able to participate in providing your viewpoint on pending legislation. Keep in frequent contact, support them, and let them know when you need help. You don't have to tell them when you help them—the good ones know it. You can pursue similar strategies whether you want to work with the leader of your local county, your governor, or your state's U.S. senator.

Understand that there are some politicians who will take your money but not your calls. Understand that there are other politicians who will take your money and do anything. I'm not talking about either. In America, politicians want to get elected and then they want to get reelected. In between, many of them want to do good. Your job is to connect with these politicians and create the environment in which you can demonstrate to them you also want to do good. An effective government relations program gives you the opportunity to be heard and the chance to positively influence your government.

You're not going to get any special favors, at least not from anyone you would want to deal with. You are more likely to be treated fairly. An investigation is less likely to drag on endlessly. You're more likely to get a fair hearing of your story. If you're concerned about legislation, you should get a meeting when it really counts. In short, a good program gets you a seat at the table.

Like many companies, Howie's tried to put it off. But you can't start a government relations program when you're already in trouble. Howie ended up spending hundreds of thousands of dollars and countless hours complying with the State's investigation. He spent much more fending off a class action lawsuit. Howie and I spent virtually every waking minute for a month preparing for a Senate hearing. Eventually, Howie and his company weathered the storm. But he lost a lot of momentum defending his company instead of building it.

Now Howie meets regularly with elected officials to get to know them and educate them about his business. He gladly attends fundraisers and is happy to contribute. Talk about a transformation. In nine states Howie's lobbyists have helped the company pass laws that are aiding his industry. Howie's still a little battle scarred and not completely out of the woods, but his business is growing again. The suitors are once more sniffing around.

But he still doesn't like opening up thick envelopes from the government.

# 19

## Don't Be a Competition Factory

*Carrots and Sticks*

I am interviewing a job candidate for a client one day, but I know within minutes he's a "no-go." Oh, sure, the guy is incredibly qualified—one of the best I've seen. But he is going to be our worst nightmare down the road. He has excellent credentials and the right experience and will fit in great. That isn't the problem. It's his response to the classic question: "Where do you see yourself in five years?" He's all warmed up by our initial chitchat and candidly responds, "I'd like to learn everything I can about the business and then start my own. Just like this company." "Interview over," I tell myself, as I imagine him falling through a hidden trapdoor in the floor.

You owe your employees respect, fair compensation, interesting work—if feasible—and a future. But you don't owe them the opportunity to copy or steal your business.

You shouldn't be in the business of creating competitors.

### The Bad, the Ugly, and the Deadly

You open your kimono, train your folks, groom them, put them in front of your clients, and even make superstars of them. Next thing you know they're competing with you. I see it all the time, the owner of a company is busy putting out fires or reeling in business or calling it in from the beach without an eye on the shop. Whatever the cause—and there are plenty—next thing he knows his right-hand man has ransacked the business. When you become a competition factory, none of it is good.

**THE BAD:** Your "go-to guy" goes. Kinda sucks. One day he's managing your top accounts. Next day he's managing your top accounts for the company across the street. It's like getting up from hours at a slot machine and having the next player win the big payoff on her first quarter.

**THE UGLY:** It can get worse. Here your mentee takes every bit of know-how that he surreptitiously leached out of you over the years, down to your best one-liners and secret handshakes. Then he sets up his own shop. Clients peel away. Your misfortune becomes his fortune. It's one giant sucker punch in the stomach and the wallet. You may never recover.

**THE DEADLY:** This one is like *Mutiny on the Bounty*. All that teamwork you fostered was good for something—your team leaves en masse. You end up with a smaller shop, or none at all, and the mutineers go on to run a copy of your old business— minus you. They've taken the big boat and left you on a dinghy.

All of these exact a terrible emotional toll on the owner, and have devastating consequences for the business. The owner feels betrayed and the practical losses hurt not only current sales and operations but also his long-term ability to sell the business.

Still some owners ignore the warning signs. And when they're smacked in the face with the unpleasant reality that thieves— masquerading as trusted employees—walked off with the family jewels, they curl up in a ball and die a little bit. Eventually they lick their wounds and recover, though many go on to make the same mistakes.

That's not the answer—nor is treating your team like the enemy. You'll never hire smart if you worry that every job candidate is a threat and you'll never get big if you fear each great employee will be a competitor. If the Colonel didn't share the seven secret spices, KFC would have been a one-joint operation. You need to hire people who are so good it hurts to lose them. But that's only half of the solution. The best and only option is to hire good and protect even better.

So you need a program of incentives and penalties—carrots and sticks, if you will—that allows you to share the knowledge, contacts, and control while protecting your business.

## Sticks

There are a number of ways to prevent your company from becoming a competition factory:

**NONCOMPETE AGREEMENTS:** This is the Louisville Slugger of the sticks, because it can hurt like hell when you hit someone with it. This agreement can keep your ex-employees from working for your competitors or starting a competing business. These restrictions cover the region around your business and usually last for one year but can be longer or shorter depending on the rules in your state. Courts enforce noncompetes to encourage you to train new employees and share important info, contacts, and customers—otherwise, you might not take the chance. Properly drafted, a noncompete can even allow you to rush into court and get an order freezing a former employee in his tracks. But they are not foolproof. Many judges refuse to enforce them. I saw one ignore a noncompete because it was Christmas Eve and the ex-employees played on the court's sympathies.

But noncompetes work. Former employees don't want to get tangled up in a fight—so they comply to avoid the stress and expense of a lawsuit. Likewise, many companies will refuse to offer a job to your ex-employee if it could get them sucked into a dispute.

Noncompetes are also indispensable to the sale of a business. Most purchasers won't pay top dollar unless your key employees are tied up. They're smart enough to make sure that what they're paying for doesn't walk out the door a week after the closing.

**CONFIDENTIALITY AGREEMENTS:** Your success may depend on keeping secrets. Whether you have formulas, client lists, or databases, a confidentiality agreement shuts the door on disclosure. These agreements are pretty airtight and will prohibit disclosure by employees—especially after they leave your company.

**COMPUTER RESTRICTIONS:** In today's world, employees can shoplift your assets any number of ways. They can steal Old School—using backpacks, the trunk of their car, or a FedEx envelope. But they can also hijack your stuff in ones and zeroes using the Internet or nonchalantly walk out the front door with a key-chain flash drive holding a few giganta bits of your intellectual property. So what's an anxious entrepreneur to do? You must monitor computer usage. Also restrict employees to using company-provided computers and phones—so you can retrieve them when the employees leave. One client let his top salesman use his own laptop. Trying to get that computer back and erase the company data was like negotiating a Middle East peace treaty.

**NONSOLICITATION AGREEMENTS:** You may need to prohibit others from offering jobs to your employees. For example, if you're a temporary placement firm, you certainly don't want customers poaching your talent—unless they pay the right fee.

Also, add a nonsolicitation clause to a noncompete agreement to stop an employee from encouraging others to leave.

These sticks have their limits. California bans noncompete agreements altogether and plenty of other states limit them. Any of these protections can be hard to enforce and some judges look for any technicality to let your employees off the hook.

Even if the sticks worked every time, you still would need the carrots. You want employees who are enticed, not trapped. You want a team that is fulfilled, not shackled. It's the only way to achieve real success. So break out the positive reinforcement.

## Carrots

You can't make attorneys sign noncompetes—it's against the law. So if you run a law firm, you don't have the crutch of that big stick. That's actually healthy because it forces you to treat people right in order to keep them.

This logic applies to any business. If your employees are bound by noncompetes, you may get lazy and take them for granted. When your folks aren't handcuffed, you're forced to think about doing what's reasonable to keep them happy. It's not a case of "Hey, they can't go anywhere. So I can treat 'em the way I want." Heck, I've seen the general manager of a TV station quit and sit on a couch in front of television at home for a year—while his noncompete expired—rather than take any more crap from the jerks at "corporate." Sticks can be necessary—and quite effective. But add carrots and you've found the best way to avoid being a competition factory.

## Retention—Not Detention

What makes people stay? Money and benefits don't hurt. But if you reward longevity, you'll turbo-charge retention. For example, paid vacation should increase the longer an employee stays with your company. Your employees should "vest" or earn certain perks—such as stock options and matching 401(k) payments—once they have notched a certain number of years with your company.

But anybody can top your pay and perks—all it takes is a checkbook. You can show you're special—heck, you can blow the competition out the water—by creating a stable, secure work environment, letting people work on projects they enjoy, and showing respect. It's not as crazy as it sounds—and it works.

Most of all, find out what makes your employees tick. You're never going to know if you don't talk with them. If you discover their aspirations, you can help them realize their dreams—at your company.

## Should You Be Institutionalized?

No matter what, you are going to get a divorce from some of your employees. If you want to minimize competition from your ex—and win the custody battle over your customers—you need to build customer loyalty.

Institutionalization is the key. It's a fancy way of saying that you want your customers to bond with your company, not individual employees. Don't get me wrong. It's fine—and may even be great—if your customers love your employees. You just don't want them to love your employee and leave you—when the employee goes. If Harry quits his job as a salesman in the Men's Department at Nordstrom, he'd better not take half of the department's customers—at least that's what Nordstrom hopes.

How do you institutionalize your business? First, create a strong brand, just like Nordstrom. When you think of Nordstrom, you envision legendary service, such as their "no questions asked" return policy. This is no accident. Nordstrom has worked hard to roll out the red carpet for their customers. Why would any customers give that up even if their favorite employee left for Bloomingdale's?

Next you want multiple people at your company working with each customer. That way the departure of one employee won't be a big letdown for your customers.

Then go the extra mile to make the sum greater than the parts. Put your company in a position to do things that no one employee can provide. Companies do it all the time with loyalty programs that provide points, discounts, or even your eleventh smoothie free.

## Open for Business—Not Competitors

Most people learn by scars—once burned, twice shy. This is one lesson that you don't want to learn the hard way. I've seen the carnage when an ambitious mentee grabs the playbook and steals a bunch of clients. It's not pretty—it can crush the spirit and even the survival of your business. Put as much effort and ingenuity into protecting your company as you do into growing it. Don't be a competition factory.

# 20

## Letting Go

### *Can You?*

Harry looked like hell. He sat across the conference table, unshaven, eyes bloodshot, hair mussed, hands trembling, and jaw working wordlessly—looking like somebody was about to find a body in the trunk of his car. He got up and sat back down a few times, drummed his fingers on the tabletop, and started to talk but didn't. He had called first thing that morning and begged me to clear my schedule and meet him immediately. He was at my office in minutes. His business is across town, so he must have been parked nearby waiting for me to get in.

"Harry, what's going on? I'm not a criminal attorney—you know that," I said.

"Nnnn-no, no, no. It's not that." He finally spoke. "Worse."

"What? What's going on? I've never seen you like this before. Harry, tell me."

"I'm thinking of selling the business."

I have worked with plenty of people who sold their businesses. You'd think they would be thrilled about getting an offer, but instead they were worried about everything. They were understandably concerned about what would happen to their employees, as well as the business itself. But they were also inexplicably agitated over less monumental issues, like whether the purchaser was showing proper respect or the hassle of organizing files and gathering paperwork or whether the closing would take place at their office or the purchaser's.

Whether they knew it or not, the decision to sell really turned on two essential questions, one predictable and the second a big mystery. As you would expect, the first was the money question. How much will I get? The second and more important question was often unspoken but ate away at them. What will I do with myself after I have sold?

Business owners have plenty of reasons for selling, including grim ones, anything from burnout, to bad health, to a changing world that is forcing them to do business in new—and undesirable—ways. Then there are the happy business owners who get an offer they simply can't refuse. Here you sell even though you love your job, your colleagues, and your business. Whether or not the joy is gone, if a purchaser offers any of these folks enough money and they can figure out who they will be without their business, they'll sell.

Harry had built a business that had turned into his own little cash factory. At first competitors tried to buy him out but made lowball offers. He ignored them. Then national players stepped in and the money got serious—real serious. He finally got his dream offer—more than any reasonable person could ask for and minimal strings attached. But instead of rapture, he had heartburn. He felt disoriented. He couldn't sleep. Jolts of fears struck him out of nowhere. He even got weepy watching TV commercials. By the morning we met in my office, he was a wreck and didn't know why.

Harry didn't have an answer for that second question—he didn't know what he would do with his life if he sold. Most entrepreneurs aren't capable of building a business without going all in—without putting all of their chips on the table. Sure, Harry had a wife and kids, and he planned to get to know them someday. Friends, well, he didn't have any who weren't on the payroll. Hobbies? Ha!

So it was all about the business. And that would go away if he sold, which turned out to be a very scary prospect. His company was so much a part of him that Harry hadn't introduced himself to anyone in the last few decades without mentioning the business—as if it was who he was, not what he did. He was physically ill at the very thought of not having the company. He felt loss, not accomplishment.

What happens when you don't overcome these feelings? What happens when you can't let go? You sabotage the deal. You come up with reasons for not selling or disrupt the process:

- You don't want to sell because you don't like the buyers—as if that matters.

- You don't read the contract for the sale of your business even though you have had it for weeks. In that time, you read *Sports Illustrated* cover-to-cover, helped your kids with their homework for the first time in years, and joined your wife in baking cookies. Is someone avoiding something?

- You're happy with the price, but you tried to raise it anyway.

- You're offended—no, no, indignant—about the buyer's purchase agreement, even though your consultants assure you it's all normal.

Harry was never going to be the beach guy or the fly-fishing guy. He couldn't sit around the house all day watching television or go to the movies or spend every night having a long fancy meal in a restaurant. To Harry, vacations were all about recharging your batteries so you could throw yourself back into work.

Maybe if Harry had been a couple of decades older, he would gladly just sail off into retirement. He might not even have had any trepidation about selling his company. If you go to dinner or a country club in Palm Beach, you'll find plenty of ex–Captains of Industry yelling at waiters about spotted spoons or gladly golfing off years of steering the ship. Despite missing a few of the trappings of power, these sellers were comfortable retiring.

Harry was too young and energetic to retire, but he finally worked through his fears. We talked it out for days. Instead of continuing to beat on himself, with a little encouragement he started appreciating the positives. He accepted the fact that the sale would give him the financial security that he had always wanted for his family and himself. Better still, instead of trying to learn to love golf, he would start another business. He would also have a nice nest egg to get the new venture launched. This time he would learn from all the mistakes of the past. If we kept his noncompete agreement with the purchaser relatively short—say, six months, a year at most—Harry would be ready to start a new venture in no time.

Other entrepreneurs, a rare few, go to work for the purchaser. These tend to be the ones who sell early, usually because they're tired of all the hassles or have run out of cash. They need the resources of a bigger enterprise to survive or bring their company to the next level. They don't mind—or have no choice but to accept the fact—that they won't be in charge anymore. For them, selling is the best and only option.

There are some who can't walk away. They're staying with the ship—above or below the water. They can't let go.

If you can't let go, you'll never sell your business. That's not bad—it's a choice. Plenty of entrepreneurs enjoy their business too much to give up the helm. But the goal here, in this book, is to build and sell your business. You have to realize that building your business is the means and selling it is an end—but not the end of you.

# 21

## For Sale

### An Overview

Have you figured out what you want out of life? Well, it's decision time.

Out of nowhere, you just got a real offer from someone who wants to buy your company. It's not perfect, though it is tempting and a damn good start. The problem is you don't know the first thing about selling your business. But if you hesitate, you may lose the opportunity forever.

Don't freak out. Remember that getting to this point is like making it to the Olympics. Selling your business will be like winning the Gold. You should be proud just getting to the games. Enjoy. Take great pleasure in your success. As usual, let that soak in for a good thirty seconds before you move on to the next challenge.

Here it is. You've got a lot to learn, and new skills will be critical to your success. Selling involves win-lose decisions. When you built your business, the process was much more forgiving. You could learn from your mistakes and they didn't put you out of business. Selling isn't like that. You build your business over years, but you might sell it in months. You don't have time to recover from your mistakes. One wrong move and you get a lot less for your company.

Then there are the buyers. They have a lot of money but usually don't part with it easily. They're smart and most have bought a lot of businesses. In fact, that's often their business—buying businesses.

They're good at it. They eat rookies for breakfast. They love nothing more than buying on the cheap. This is not the time to rely on the kindness of strangers.

Then there's you. You need the restraint to steer clear of shortcuts and the insight to avoid pitfalls. You need the discipline to maximize your return and not react to the moment.

But don't worry. Unlike sex, you can do it right the first time. It's worth it. The difference between winging it and working it can be tens of millions of dollars.

It doesn't have to be mysterious. There is a science and art to selling. There is a process. It's all part of a winning program.

## The Winning Program

First, here is a wake-up call, a slap in the face, a gut check—whatever you want to call it: *don't enter into this process halfheartedly*. There is a tremendous cost in just trying to sell your business—in the time and energy of you and your colleagues, in the extraordinary fees you will pay the professionals assisting you, and in the blow to company morale if the deal falls through. Think carefully about starting the process. Consult with experienced professionals to get a preview of the likely results.

Be realistic. Selling your company is difficult. If you're not up for it, you will do a bad job and get a bad result or you'll give up before you finish—and that's worse than not starting at all.

If this chapter even slightly discourages you from trying to sell your business, stop now. Save the trees. Wait until you are ready.

Second, assemble your deal team. Selling successfully involves having the right players, from investment bankers, to lawyers and accountants, to your own executives. These are the people who are going to help you find potential buyers, tout your company, and negotiate and document the sale. If that's not enough pressure, you may be working with some of these people for the first time—because your everyday lawyer or accountant might not be the right expert for the job. Your deal will be only as good as they are—so get references, interview the candidates, and pick wisely.

Third, you need a plan. Don't shoot from the hip. Sit down with your team and map out the selling process—including the players, their roles, and a schedule. Establish lines of authority—who is the boss of whom. Bruised egos are better than anarchy and confusion.

You will also need to consider some key questions. Are you willing to sell all of your company, part of it, or are you flexible? If you sell, would you stay on and work for the purchaser?

Timing is crucial, too. You just can't sell when you feel like it. The market has to be right. You get a better deal when lenders are throwing money at borrowers, and you have little chance of getting any deal when loans have dried up. Best of all, jump on a mania. At the beginning of the dot-com boom, investors were throwing crazy money at virtually any business that was on the Net and had "eyeballs." Your plan has to have enough structure to guide you but enough flexibility to seize opportunities.

Fourth, you will make mistakes, but you need to avoid the ones that cost millions of dollars or even the deal itself. For many, this will be the first and only business they ever sell. Even if you sold a business before, you're only human. Avoid the biggest mistake of all—losing your bargaining power:

**DON'T COUNT ON SELLING:** Run your business like you're never selling it—until the day you close on the sale. If you take your eye off the ball, the value of your business could crater and the seller may renegotiate or walk away.

**HAVE ALTERNATIVES:** Get as many potential buyers involved as possible and don't commit until you have the one you want.

**DON'T BE TOO EAGER:** If you fall in love with the idea of selling, buyers will think you're desperate and lowball you. As with a lot of things in life, you have play hard to get.

Fifth, and finally, this is difficult. Selling is invasive. It makes a prostate exam feel like a pat on the back. Selling is uncertain. Buyers walk away for all kinds of reasons and sometimes right on the wedding day. Selling is an endurance test. Buyers stall to weaken your resolve and see if your business stays strong. Prepare for these challenges. You'll get a better deal.

You only get to sell your business once—do it right.

# 22

# Key Terminology: 101

## *Talking the Talk*

Victor was great at building his business. But he didn't know the first thing about selling it. Worse, he wouldn't admit it. He was so afraid of looking like a rookie, he almost gave away the company.

His blunder came when he met with a prospective buyer before Victor knew what he was doing. After the normal pleasantries, the buyer finally cleared his throat, suppressed a smirk, and said, "We really like this business, so we're offering you five times EBITDA."

Victor had a puzzled look on his face. But before I could cut him off, he thrust his hand out to shake and quickly proclaimed, "That sounds good. You got a deal!"

Then, as I buried my head in my hands, Victor tilted toward me and whispered, "What's EBITDA?"

You don't want to look stupid—especially when you're trying to sell your business for a lot of money. But selling has its own lingo and there is power in knowing the jargon. The buyers and investors pawing over your business aren't volunteering fair deals, and you're not going to ask for something if you've never heard of it. They also aren't going to be bashful about what they want and you might not object if you don't understand. So here's a quick primer on the key terms:

**"BAD BOY" PROVISIONS:** When you sell, you make all kinds of representations and agreements about how you built and operated your company. For example, you might represent that you have all of the licenses you need to operate your business. Usually you are not personally liable if those promises are broken. So if you didn't have a necessary license, the buyer would have remedies but not be able to go after your house, bank account, or other personal assets. However, some behavior is so bad that if it comes back to haunt the purchaser, you will be personally liable for it. These sins are described in the *"bad boy"* provisions. They usually include failing to pay your taxes, committing fraud, and spilling hazardous materials. If you violate a bad boy provision, you're personally on the hook for any harm the buyer suffers as a result.

**BREAKUP FEE:** In any sale, buyers and sellers spend a lot of time and a ton of money on things like legal, accounting, and investment-banking fees. They also pass up other deals while they're working on yours. Because so much is devoted to the deal, some buyers—and even some sellers—insist that if the other side walks away, it must pay a fee for breaking up. Sometimes a *breakup fee* is also payable if the parties can't get necessary government or other approval for the sale.

**CAPITALIZATION:** While capitalization is a rough measure of a company's value, it is frequently used to give you a sense of a company's size. Capitalization equals the sum of a business' long-term debt *plus* the value of its stock (or other equity interests, such as LLC membership interests) *plus* its retained earnings. But if a company is publicly traded, people instead look at the "market capitalization" of the business—which equals the company's outstanding stock multiplied by the current price for one share. For instance, "small cap" refers to a public company that is relatively small in size, when measured by the value of all of its outstanding stock.

**DISCOUNTED CASH FLOW:** Discounted cash flow analysis is a sophisticated two-step process for estimating a company's value. First, estimate the cash that the business will generate each year—technically forever. Second, figure out how much all of that money is worth today. That is the discounting part. In calculating that discount, you need to consider what inflation does to reduce the value of money over time, the risk that you won't even get the money, and the fact that you won't be able to use some of that money for a long while. In short, the discounted cash flow is a measure of how much cash the business will generate—forever—but discounted to the amount that a reasonable person would accept in order to get it all up front. It's like a lottery paying the winner a lump sum of $4 million cash up front instead of $10 million over many years.

**DUE DILIGENCE:** Buyers have two approaches to making sure they are getting what they expect when they purchase a business. In one method, they make the seller sign a contract that's about two feet thick and contains every conceivable promise you can dream up. In the other approach, due diligence, they examine the company very thoroughly. The buyers interview employees, customers, and even government regulators, review company contracts and business records, and then physically inspect factories, offices, stores, or wherever else the seller does business. Some buyers emphasize one approach over the other and still others combine both—like mixing torture and imprisonment.

**EBITDA:** Buyers want to understand what a business really earns. They also want to compare the earnings of different companies—apples-to-apples—so they can decide which to buy. A business' taxable income provides some information—but it's misleading. For example, taxable income is reduced by things like depreciation of equipment, which is really just a tax write-off in some cases and not a true expense that you shell out money for. Or, in another situation, a company may have borrowed a lot of money while a competitor didn't borrow any. Even if both businesses have the same revenues, the one that borrows will end up with lower taxable income because it will deduct interest expenses.

For these reasons, buyers want to know your EBITDA. EBITDA is your *Earnings Before* you deduct *Interest, Taxes, Depreciation,* and *Amortization.* EBITDA lets a buyer know how much a company really earns without the distortions caused by deductions that are often irrelevant to the value of a business.

If only Victor had known. Sure, his numbers were great—he had just cracked $20 million a year in gross income. But Victor was no investment banker. He thought revenue was the same as EBITDA and that he was being offered five times that, or $100 million. But even though EBITDA includes interest, taxes, depreciation, and amortization, it still deducts payroll, rent, cost of goods, and every other expense. Victor's $20 million gross shriveled to $3 million of EBITDA. The offer of five times EBITDA translated that $3 million into a $15 million sale (which is nice but not $100 million!). Victor nearly fainted when I explained his misunderstanding. After the blood slowly returned to Victor's face, he mumbled an apology to the buyer and asked for his company back.

**GAAP:** Generally Accepted Accounting Principles (GAAP). What could sound more ordinary and nonthreatening? Guess again. GAAP is a complicated, complex, and strict set of accounting rules established by a variety of organizations, such as the Financial Accounting Standards Board (FASB). They're like the Darth Vaders of the accounting world. They tell you that you can't deduct the expense of your new Web site— instead you need to write it off over a number of years. GAAP statements provide a lot more detail, require rigorous analysis, and produce financial statements with a lot less room for "creative accounting"—although there is still some wiggle room for interpretation. If your company is a start-up or a small company, you're not preparing your financial statements in accordance with GAAP. Once you get large, borrow a lot of money, or go public, you'll need GAAP statements and you'll pay a bundle to get them prepared by experts. In the meantime, don't promise to give anyone GAAP statements until you know exactly what is required.

**INVESTMENT BANKER:** An investment banker is essentially a business broker, but with a much better suit and bigger brain. They've got great charts and silver tongues and the best of them can sell sand at the beach.

**MAC:** Material Adverse Change (MAC). Most buyers agree to purchase your business based on your current success. If one of your major customers cancels their contract with you, that would be a MAC and the seller could call off the purchase.

## Selling Part of Your Company

Sometimes you sell part of your company on the way to selling all of it. Other times you bring in an investor to raise cash and stay alive or fund growth. The following terms apply when you have a new member of the family—the co-owner.

**ANTI-DILUTION:** When investors buy a stake in your company, they are concerned that you might sell more stock to others at a lower price. These additional sales at reduced prices drive down the average value of each share of company stock. For this reason, the investors often get anti-dilution rights that restrict your ability to sell company stock below a certain price. These are enormously complicated provisions that demand attention because they can hamstring your future growth and give too much control to investors by limiting your options.

**CLAWBACK:** A clawback right allows one party—usually the investor—to get something back if the other party does not perform as promised. For example, an investor might require that you—the founder—enter into a formal employment agreement with your company that gives you a base salary and bonuses. But the bonuses from one year can be clawed back if earnings fall off a cliff in the next year.

**COVENANTS:** Technically, a covenant is just another promise. But to your co-owner, the "covenants"—especially the financial covenants—are the most important promises in the deal. For example, a classic covenant—the "net working capital" requirement—assures an investor that your company has a minimum amount of cash on hand. The savvy investor wants to know that your company isn't running out of money any time soon.

**DRAG-ALONG:** Investors who buy a stake in your company usually want to resell that stake in three to seven years. But often they can't sell that stake alone. Plenty of buyers won't purchase anything less than 100 percent of a business. So the investors need to be able to *drag-along* your piece of the company and sell the whole business. If you're smart, you'll refuse to sell unless this sale meets your needs, such as an all-cash sale or one with a minimum selling price.

On the flip side, some investors find a buyer who only wants to buy part of your company. Here you need to make sure that you have *tag-along* rights that enable you to sell your stock, too.

**MEZZANINE DEBT:** Mezzanine debt is similar to a second mortgage on your house. The first mortgage gets paid off first and carries a lower interest rate because the lender takes less risk—there is usually ample equity in your house to pay the first loan. The second mortgage is a riskier proposition and you have to pay more for it because the second lender could get wiped out in a foreclosure. That's where mezzanine debt gets its name, from the second, or "mezzanine," level of repayment.

Just like home loan lenders, the banks financing business purchases limit their risks and often won't lend the full purchase price. So mezzanine lenders fill an important gap in many business acquisitions by providing a chunk of the money to buy your business. When you're selling your entire company, the mezzanine lender is mostly the purchaser's headache. But when you're only selling part, teammate, it's your problem, too.

By the way, any debt—including mezzanine debt—that is paid after other loans is also called *subordinated debt.*

**PIGGYBACK:** Some investors who buy a piece of your company want to further grow the business and then sell their stock in an initial public offering (IPO). What a lot of entrepreneurs don't realize is that these investors may make arrangements to sell their stock—but not yours—so they get to cash out and you get to stay home cleaning the floors for your wicked stepmother. The key is to make sure that when these investors register their stock so that it can be sold publicly, they also register your stock. You want to piggyback on their registration. Otherwise, have fun with the floors.

**RATCHET UP:** Investors will try to pin you down and turn your rosy projections of future income into binding promises of future performance. Then, if you don't hit those "guaranteed" numbers, the investors will want to increase or *ratchet up* their ownership of your company. So a 10 percent investor stake in your company might ratchet up to a 20 percent holding if you don't hit your numbers.

No one likes going to a fancy dinner only to find out he's on the menu. Now that you know what these terms mean, you can enjoy the feast instead of being the main course.

If you want to walk the walk, you've got to talk the talk.

# 23

# Investment Bankers

## Dealing with the Deal Makers

You've worked your heart out for years building your company. Don't blow it now. Whether you're selling or just raising money, you need to assemble a team with the talents to get the deal done. A critical member of your team is the right matchmaker—the investment banker—to find the buyer or investor and help close the deal.

You know the value of a good matchmaker if you've dealt with a bad one like:

- The dating service that sets you up with someone who has the same stalking tendencies as an old ex—only now you don't have the protection of a restraining order

- The travel agent who books you into a "luxury" hotel where the motto is "Sorry, we're out of that"

- The real estate broker who convinces you to buy the condo-from-hell where heat, electricity, and water are periodic treats and the fire alarms work more than the elevators

The same goes when selling your company. You don't want an inept investment banker pushing you down the wedding aisle with the business equivalent of Bridezilla.

While selling takes a team, investment bankers are indispensable to finding buyers and getting your price. They're business brokers—but so much more. They advise you on when you should sell and for how much, screen buyers, and, like some revered Secretary of State, shuttle back and forth between warring parties, overcoming impasses and negotiating key terms of the deal.

With so much riding on the investment banker, find the one who "gets" you and your company, knows the players, and has the knowledge and experience to carve a path to the deal.

Understand, though, that the lions of the jungle eat people, too. It's their nature. You're dealing with expert deal makers. As ultimate negotiators, they can't help themselves. They're not just going to get a great deal *for you*. They also want a great deal *from you*. You're going to agree to pay these people a lot, maybe millions. So you need to be almost as thoughtful hammering out your deal with your investment banker as you are selling your company.

## The Role of the Investment Banker

As with any professionals, there are good investment bankers and bad ones. The best are gurus of the selling and investing game. They serve as strategic advisors, guiding you on when to sell, how to sell, and for how much. They negotiate the key terms of the deal, especially the economics.

They also serve as a buffer and mediator. Sellers can get testy when it comes to parting with their companies, and buyers and investors can get testy when it comes to parting with their money. Sometimes you have an entirely cranky bunch of people who, if left unattended, are ready to rumble in an unsanctioned Texas Death Match. The experienced investment banker will separate the parties, reinforce their shared goals, and craft compromises.

Like a good matchmaker, good investment bankers also help you show your best side. They coach you on how to talk about your company, including prepping your "one-minute elevator speech" and rehearsing answers to the most difficult questions. They also help write the "Book" about your company. This treatise describes your company, its history, and current operations, as well as financial results and projections for the future. With these props in hand, they arrange "dog and pony shows" where your deal team makes presentations to prospective buyers and investors.

You can't underestimate the value of a great investment banker. There will be countless times in any deal when you face hard decisions. Which buyer to go with? How to counter an offer? What issues are deal killers? Experienced investment bankers will add tremendous value with their insights and guidance.

Some people try to sell or raise money without an investment banker. I guess some people also do their own surgery at home. Sure, there are times and places when do-it-yourself doesn't kill you and may even save you money. But a good investment banker almost always adds more value than he or she costs you.

## Finding the Right Investment Banker

Finding a good investment banker is like seeking out any good professional. Personal recommendations are invaluable. Talk with others who have successfully sold or raised money and learn who they liked and why. Reach out to other professionals you respect—lawyers, accountants, and bankers—and get their picks. The best people in one profession often recommend the best in other professions.

Ignore fancy advertising and slick presentations. There are plenty of people whose best effort goes into roping you in, not selling your company. If you can't get a personal recommendation, meet with investment bankers and ask for a list of the last ten clients they signed up. To be clear, you are not asking for a list of references. References are selected by people trying to impress you. They aren't going to put disgruntled customers on the list. But the last ten customers they signed up—whether or not their deals closed—give you a good menu of people to talk with. By the way, if an investment banker won't give you that list, take caution.

Don't be shy about seeking out someone with whom you "click."

You're going to be in the foxhole with your investment banker. For a while—months at least—he or she is going to be your most significant other. If your investment banker does something that annoys you in that introductory meeting, you're going to want to annihilate him or her at 2:00 A.M. when he or she does it for the umpteenth time. Go for some personal chemistry.

Likewise, make sure that your investment banker works well with the rest of your deal team. This team will include some of your senior executives, as well as your outside legal and financial pros—lots of talent, but tons of ego, too. It helps to have the prospective team members meet before selections are finalized. Let them interview each other. Some creative tension is good—you don't want a bunch of yes-people. But outright warfare is counterproductive.

Finally, don't worry about getting a local player. It is much more important to get a genius who is connected and knows the buyers and investors in your field than it is to get someone who knows your company and hometown. If you have to fly in the wunderkind, do it. Search broadly and get the investment banker who makes the best deals in your industry.

## "The Deal" Before *the Deal*

Investment bankers can help you make a fortune. But if you're not careful, they can cost you one, too. One entrepreneur got a bill—and then a lawsuit—for millions of dollars from an investment banker who did little more than send a letter out to a bunch of potential buyers. I was brought in to persuade the investment banker his claim was erroneous or club him into submission—whatever got the job done.

The situation came to a boil after my client fired the original investment banker. The replacement investment banker found a buyer within months and the deal closed quickly. My client was still doing high fives with his deal team and meeting with his wealth managers when the original investment banker started making increasingly outrageous threats. He claimed that his loosely worded agreement with the seller entitled him to a fee for finding the buyer. Turns out the buyer was on the list of people who got a letter about the sale when the disgruntled investment banker was still on the job.

However fantastic this one-page letter may have been and however much he spent on postage and stationery for a few dozen letters, the simple fact is that the buyer never even read that letter. The buyer learned the company was for sale from his long-standing golf buddy, the new investment banker. We had to fight the lawsuit for a while until we convinced the original investment banker that his expectations were unrealistic and he should walk away with a token, face-saving settlement. This client escaped real damage, but he learned that the investment-banking agreement must be precise, especially about fees and how they're earned.

You need to cut the right deal with your investment banker—from the outset—or you won't maximize the sale of your company. Here are the key points:

## 1. Fees

Investment bankers typically want:

1. Guaranteed monthly fees, at least for a minimum time period, such as the first six months of the job.

2. Reimbursement of expenses.

3. A percentage of the money they get you. This is the one that can add up to millions of dollars. It is not unusual to see this percentage fee ranging anywhere from 1 to 5 percent of the amount a buyer or investor pays you for part or all of the company.

The key is to make sure these fees work for you. First, you shouldn't be locked into accepting just any deal your investment banker finds.

Retain the right to reject any deal you don't like, or establish a minimum acceptable price (keep this secret!).

Second, don't pay a lot if you don't get a lot. Often the percentage fee is structured so that the investment banker gets a higher percentage as the sales or investment proceeds increase. For example, the fee might be 1 percent of the first $100 million and 2 percent of the excess. Sometimes this structure provides many tiers, with the percentage going up four or five times as the proceeds increase.

Third, sometimes a particularly aggressive investment banker (yes, that is redundant) wants stock or warrants in your company or some other piece of the deal. Strike this provision. You're hiring the investment banker, not making him or her a partner. Absent some extraordinary circumstance, this is inappropriate. Most deals are difficult enough to close without the investment banker trying to shoehorn him- or herself into ownership of your company.

## 2. Term

How much time should you give your investment banker to find a buyer or investor? Market conditions always affect timing. Six months is ideal and nine months may be necessary. But never agree to more than one year. If your investment banker doesn't find a good buyer or investor in a year, it is time to start over. It is also smart to include some interim milestones in your agreement with the investment banker. For example, if you don't have three to five written offers within a fixed time period, you should have the right to say good-bye to your investment banker.

But be fair. Often the business owners cause delays. Your investment banker can't effectively market your company if you don't produce all of the necessary data and documents. You also have to assemble the rest of the deal team. So give your investment banker enough time to do the job right—but not more.

## 3. Investment Banker Protection Period

Savvy investment bankers want to "own" the buyers and investors they bring to you—even after their investment-banking agreement expires. Without this protection, you could wait until the agreement ends, then sell and avoid paying the investment banker. So investment bankers insist on getting paid if you do a deal with one of their buyers or investors within a fixed time period—the protection period—tacked onto the end of your agreement. This protection is fair, but make sure the investment banker has some meaningful contact with the prospect—and did not just send an e-mail blast to hundreds of possible buyers. Ideally, the prospects must have submitted a written offer to buy or invest in your company. Then limit the protection period. Six months to one year following the end of your investment-banking agreement is reasonable.

---

Investment bankers are smart and successful people. But they're not shy about what they want. They're going to hand you their "wish list" agreement. Don't sign it. It's almost like an intelligence test. If you sign it, you fail. Start practicing for the big deal by negotiating an agreement with your investment banker that works for all involved.

As talented as they are, you don't hire investment bankers just because you like them. A good one opens doors you can't, closes deals that would otherwise crumble, and makes you money.

# 24

## Surveying the Market
### *Identifying Prospective Buyers*

For a long time now, maybe from the first day you opened for business, you have had one burning question. At times of victory, it tantalized you. In moments of doubt, it dogged you. Now you are about to find out. How much will I get for selling my company?

That depends—to a surprising degree—on who's buying. As with everything else in life, some people will pay more than others for the very same thing.

Some buyers don't spend a lot but take big chances with their money.

Some buyers spend a lot but don't take any chances with their money.

Some buyers want their investment back right away and others can wait a long time.

Some buyers don't care so much about making money; they have other reasons for buying.

So if you want to know how much you're going to get, the first thing you do is survey the market of buyers and find out who's interested in a business like yours.

### Financial Versus Strategic Buyers

As the name suggests, financial buyers are all about the numbers. In contrast, strategic buyers are looking for synergy.

**FINANCIAL BUYERS:** These "number crunchers" purchase businesses like other people do stocks, with the goal of buying low and selling high. Financial buyers have learned that they can make more money flipping a good business than they can with stocks, bonds, or real estate. While the stock market has historic returns of 10 percent per year, these folks are looking to make 20 percent or more per year on their investments. Typically, they like to buy a business and hold it for three to seven years. In that time period, if company earnings have shot up, they cash out by either selling the business or taking it public. Expect them to be rigorous in their analysis of your earnings, now and in the future.

**STRATEGIC BUYERS:** These buyers are not looking to make money in the narrow sense of flipping companies for a profit. They want businesses that add synergy or some special edge. A strategic buyer might be a home builder that purchases a timber company to nail down a steady supply of lumber and mountaintop sites for new resorts. Or it could be a pharmaceutical manufacturer that wants double the juice for the same old squeeze. They buy another drugmaker and then get their existing sales force to sell twice as many drugs as before. A strategic buyer can even be your competitor. Who wouldn't want to seize new customers and sales, knock out the competition, and drive up prices? Strategic buyers often pay more than financial buyers because they expect your business to create synergy and pay off in multiple ways that trump just the value of your earnings.

## Risk Takers

Some buyers will accept a lot of risk, but they want to be rewarded for it. Others won't accept as much risk and they understand that the payoff will be lower. How does that affect you? The more risk the buyers take, the more reward they demand—and you end up with a lower sales price.

So higher risk equals lower sales price. And vice versa. The less risk to the buyer, the more money you get. Here's how you look at buyers based on their willingness or refusal to accept risk:

**ANGEL INVESTORS:** They take the most risk. They invest early, when a business is in its infancy. Their investment target may be little more than two Ph.D.'s and a patent. Angels rarely buy you out entirely, because without the founders there is no business. But these guys are the "roulette wheel" players of investors. When they put their money down, they want to know they will win big if their number hits. Expect them to put in a few hundred thousand dollars or even a few million yet take the lion's share of your business.

**VENTURE CAPITALISTS:** The "VCs" still take a lot of risk, but they usually want to invest in a fully operational—if not profitable—business. You have to demonstrate that your business works, even though you are not yet reliably making money and may not have made any money at all. Again, the VCs are not likely to buy your entire company. Instead they usually want a controlling interest and then handcuff you to your desk. Also, most of the money they pay must stay in the business to fund growth, although they might let you take a little off the table so you can drive in style to your twenty-hour workdays.

**PRIVATE EQUITY/INVESTMENT COMPANIES:** These companies buy the best and pay the most. They go by a variety of names, such as private equity companies and private invest-ment companies, and they make all kinds of acquisitions and investments. But their sweet spots include buying companies with $100 million or more in annual revenues and reliably increasing income. These acquisitions are less risky for the buyer and more lucrative for the seller. If building and selling your business is a beauty contest, you get the crown, roses, and riches from these buyers.

## When Bigger Is Better

In addition to other ways of slicing and dicing buyers, the size of the buyer is a good predictor of the amount they will pay. The bigger the better:

**MOM-AND-POP BUYERS:** The little guys who buy a business want to earn their money back in three to five years. That means if you are generating $1 million a year in income, they will pay $3 to $5 million for your business. They just aren't willing to work a long time to get their money back. If it isn't already obvious, you only sell to them if you have to.

**REGIONAL PLAYERS:** Regional or midsize companies have more patience to see their investments pay off. They can wait five to ten years before they make their money back. So if you provide that same $1 million of net income, they pay $5 to $10 million. This is not Plan A. But it's still worth celebrating when you sell a company for five to ten times annual earnings.

**NATIONAL AND PUBLICLY TRADED COMPANIES:** These are the blue-chip buyers. They want it all. But they pay a lot. They are going to insist that you have reliable profits, a competitive edge, scalability, sustainability, bench strength, and everything else that makes a company strong. But they pay $10 million or more for every $1 million of your annual income. Selling to them is winning the Olympics, the Trifecta, and the Super Bowl.

## Egg Hunts, Wild-Goose Chases, and Grid Searches

Selling the right way doesn't just happen.

Selling shouldn't be some random act. If you just "let it happen," you end up with a distress sale in the flea market of the business world. Selling should be the culmination of a well-thought-out plan. From the start, build a company that will appeal to the right buyers. Every major decision should factor in what will make your company more—or less—attractive to those buyers.

One client approached me about growing and selling his business. Early on, we identified who would pay the most for the business—two publicly traded companies. As his business grew, he added products, hired employees, and built systems that would integrate with either buyer. He also added new locations that filled in geographic gaps for these buyers. It wasn't all he thought about, but building a company that would be desirable to either purchaser influenced the major decisions.

In the end, when my client decided to sell, the company was like a glove that fit the hand of one of these buyers. The purchase price was enormous because the business was so valuable to that buyer. My client could have run it forever and never made as much money as he did selling the business to the right buyer.

The lesson: if selling is your goal, your true customer is the one who buys your business.

# 25

# The Price

*Valuation Methods Versus Your Guess*

*Is as Good as Mine*

K ill it," Kent said to me.

"What the [bleep]?" I replied.

"Yeah, kill it. I'm tired of this buyer. I don't want to sell to them," Kent said, completely exasperated. He was walking away from tens of million of dollars.

I had been negotiating the sale of Kent's business. A big equity firm had dangled a lot of money in front of Kent. But they chipped away at the payoff with each round of negotiations. The payday also receded further and further away as the buyer kept kicking the tires. Then Kent got really bad news. The government canceled one of his big contracts. The buyer had already been torturing us with issues, questions, and requests, and now they were certain to lower the price again or walk away. If we were lucky, we'd get dinged for a couple of million dollars. If we weren't, the deal would die.

Kent was kaput. He was sick of the buyer, sick of the process, sick of the deal. He was tired of the never-ending examination of his books, the document requests, and the disruptive interviews of his employees. The final straw was the snide remarks from the buyer's team suggesting that Kent didn't know how to run his business.

"Kill it," Kent said again. "They're going to make me take a haircut on the sales price anyways. So, kill it. We'll take a break and try to sell it next year—for our price."

You can talk to all of the experts and they will give you their formulas for how much you're going to get for your businesses. But that only goes so far. Selling is science and happenstance. Stuff happens. Deals crater on the eve of closings. You can build your business for years, but you won't really know for sure how much you're getting for it until the wire transfer hits your bank account.

Once Kent was willing to kill the deal, everything changed—even the price tag.

## Fundamental Valuation Methods

So how do you know if you're getting the right price? You don't. But here are some clues. There are three fundamental ways to value anything:

1. Replacement cost

2. Comparable value

3. The income method

1. *Replacement Cost.* Replacement cost is the amount of money a purchaser would spend to duplicate your business. If you own a satellite radio network, the purchaser looks at the value of your broadcast licenses, the satellites you have in orbit, your ground-based infrastructure, and other assets, such as your subscription contracts with consumers. Mostly, replacement cost puts a price tag on your assets, not your income.

This valuation method is rarely used as the prime way of valuing a business. More often it is a just a factor used to justify a purchase price. When purchasers can't otherwise defend paying the sales price, they might look to replacement cost as a way to bolster the valuation.

An unprofitable satellite radio business might still be very valuable to a purchaser who wants to avoid years expanding into a new market. The buyer can safely bet that paying replacement cost is a cheap way to jump into the new market. Ample replacement cost also helps the buyer get financing for the purchase. Many lenders rely on the assets of the acquired company as collateral for the loan to the buyer.

Usually, you're going to be talking about replacement cost when business is bad and you're facing a distress sale. If all goes well, replacement cost won't be a big part of your selling discussions.

2. *Comparable Value.* Comparable value places a sales price on a business based on what other similar businesses have sold for. For example, if you are selling a franchised business that is virtually identical to hundreds of other franchises, the sales prices of similar deals would heavily influence your sales price. But most businesses vary a lot from one another. The sales price of one business usually doesn't apply to another. So comparable value is another method that has limited use in selling businesses.

3. *The Income Method.* The best and most common way to value a business is the "income method." Here virtually every buyer first tries to figure out how much the business makes now and will in the future. Then each buyer applies their own secret formula to determine how much they will pay for that stream of money. For example, one buyer might look at the average annual earnings for the past three years and pay ten times that amount. Another buyer might forecast the earnings into the future and then figure what that would all be worth to them now.

But get this: it's like a very misleading first date. They're not going to share any of that with you. Instead they sweet-talk you with a convincing-sounding speech that has an entirely different formula—or no formula at all—so they can try to buy your business for less.

You need to know what they're thinking, so you can get the most for your business. So here's what's on their minds.

## Don't Cry For Me, EBITDA

Let's start with a refresher on EBITDA. EBITDA is your annual earnings before interest, taxes, depreciation, and amortization. Basically, EBITDA is earnings that count to buyers—without things that don't matter to buyers and excluding things that make one business hard to compare to another.

Now, a lot of buyers will pay a certain multiple of your EBITDA. It is common to hear buyers talk—among themselves, not in front of their dates—about paying $x$ times EBITDA. Of course, sellers get together and wonder if the buyer will pay $y$ times EBITDA.

Other buyers determine how much they will pay based on the discounted cash flow formula. This formula starts with your current cash flow, projects how much it will increase each year, and then values how much all of that money is worth today. For example, they might figure out that your cash flow is $500,000 per year now, it will increase approximately 10 percent per year, and this river of money is worth $x$ millions of dollars today.

Well, what's a seller to do? How do you figure out what that $x$ should be?

First, try to find out what each prospective buyer has paid for other companies. If the buyer is publicly traded, you may be able to get your hands on what they paid for other companies. If you have the revenue and expense information for these other companies, your team may be able to figure out a rough idea of the formula that the buyer is using.

Second, find out the formulas used by other buyers—not yours—to buy businesses similar to yours. Your investment banker and other advisors should have examples of similar deals. When your advisors worked on those deals, they may have agreed to keep information confidential. But without revealing names, they can show you the purchase formulas that were used. In fact, one great reason for picking a particular investment banker and other advisors is their intimate knowledge of similar deals.

## On the Other Hand . . . the Wild Cards

Buying based on a multiple of your EBITDA or your discounted cash flow, or a combination of them, is common. But there are almost as many buying formulas as there are buyers. Remember strategic buyers? They might purchase a business without much regard for its earnings. Instead they could be focused on how much your business helps their existing company—and you may never be able to predict how much that's worth to the buyer.

Even when a buyer has a formula, it is going to add or take away dollars based on a variety of factors. Some of the critical things that increase your sales price include:

- A profitable business model that generates increasing EBITDA every year—all the better if it does so in a predictable fashion

- A competitive edge that keeps out the competition

- Scalability that enables the buyer to continue growing your business

- An executive team in place that can run the show without you

There are plenty of other factors that add value depending on your business—from a strong brand, to long-term contracts that tie up your customers, to risk management strategies that will reduce the buyer's downside.

Then you have to look outside your business and see what's going on in the world. During the dot-com boom some crazy investors cut deals on cocktail napkins and paid tens of millions of dollars for businesses that didn't have any paying customers, much less earnings. These investors ignored Old School businesses and were determined to throw their money at the next shiny new thing. That turned out well, didn't it?

There are other wild cards. They can ding the sales price like a dent in a car or juice the dollars like a good old-fashioned Wall Street bonus. Are people eager to buy businesses or reluctant? Are banks providing buyers with lots of money at low interest rates? Or has the lending world turned off the faucet? All of this affects how much buyers will pay.

## The Bottom Line

Don't look for a silver bullet. Get a good team and put your heads together. With the right players, you should have a rough idea of what buyers are paying and what you can do to enhance that payoff.

The bottom line is that if you have a skilled team, you get the most the buyer has to give—and that's all you should expect.

That is exactly what we wanted to do for Kent. Kent didn't know it yet, but we had just learned that—despite appearances—the buyer was getting desperate to do a deal. It was a new investment company and their first two deals had died. The buyer's parent company was fed up and threatening to shut down the whole operation if they didn't close a deal soon. It was time to squeeze the buyer, not cave in to them.

So when Kent told me to kill the deal, I told him this was our opportunity to get the deal he wanted. Kent had been so eager to sell that he had been chasing the buyer—and getting beaten up in the process. If we finally showed some brinkmanship and walked away—and really hammed it up in the process—the buyer's fear of losing the deal would overcome their greed for a bargain.

"Kent, here's the wild card," I said. "They want this deal more than you can imagine." Kent's obsession with the deal had overshadowed everything—including the buyer's own desperation to finally buy something. I explained to Kent that the buyer had sold their investors on Kent's business and spent a fortune in fees and couldn't afford to lose another deal. That would be strike three. If Kent walked away, *everything* would change: "They'll quit screwing around and close right away. No price reduction. Instead, they'll pay more—not less. Then you'll do the deal, right?"

"Jack, I just lost one of my biggest contracts and I get more, not less?" Kent smiled for the first time in weeks. "Why didn't you say so before?"

I told the attorney on the other side that Kent was finally fed up with the buyer's antics and the deal was dead. Dead, dead, dead. I was packing up my files. Nice knowing you. He did not take it well. He was still yelling as I wished him "good night" and gently put down the receiver.

The buyer wasn't about to let this deal die. They sent out the big guns. The next morning, a chauffeur delivered the buyer's CEO to my door. From his extremely conciliatory and awkwardly delivered comments it was obvious he was dying to avoid another Dead Deal Debacle. I was blunt. Kent was beyond frustration with the lengthy negotiations, the chiseling at the sales price, and the invasive manhandling of his business. Kent could live—happily—without the deal. The buyer had to woo Kent back. It would take a higher price—regardless of the lost contract—and a quick closing: "You've met Kent. He's a restless guy—and now he's a pissed-off guy. You want this business, this is the only way to buy it."

"Done," the CEO agreed.

We closed within weeks and at the right price—not the $25 million that the buyer tried to arm-twist Kent into accepting. Because he stopped chasing the deal and instead made the buyer do some running, Kent cleared millions more than he ever expected—with a $32 million purchase price.

Pricing your business involves formulas and logic. There are sure things—profitability, a competitive edge, scalability, and a great team—that get you more money. But the world around you is chaotic and fickle. Sometimes you win the game with a wild card.

# 26

# The Book on Your Business

*What Your Company Needs*

*to Be a Bestseller*

In acting, you need the right headshot to get an audition. For college admission, you have to have stellar test scores and a touchy-feely essay. To win a big contract, you must number-crunch a bid and submit a proposal that shows you're better and cheaper. And if you want to sell your business, you've got to write the Book. It's your story, heavy on the facts and figures.

If it's done right, the Book proves it would be the crime of the century not to buy your company. If it's done wrong, someone steals your business.

## The Book

You've heard the expression "You only have one chance to make a first impression." Well, this is it. Your first—and maybe only—opportunity to get a stranger interested in buying your company.

The Book is your brochure on steroids. Where you came from, who you are, and where you're going. Most of all, it is a sales pitch with proof. Here is the basic table of contents:

- Company History

- Players: The Executive Team

- Business Model

- Financials

- Forecasts and the Future

There's no mystery to these topics. They are what they sound like. "The company was founded in 2002. Bill is our software guy." Blah. Blah. Blah. The meat is your financials. Like a guy flipping through *Playboy* for the pictures, most buyers jump to the numbers. If you give them visions of dollar signs dancing in their heads, they'll go back and read the words.

For the first draft, you divvy up the writing based on expertise and experience. If the founder can still hold a pencil, he writes up the history of the company and a description of the business model. HR lifts the bios off the Web site and tackles the chapter on the players. Usually this is about your executive team but also includes anyone critical to your success. If, for example, you have a team of scientists who aren't executives but are a big part of your competitive edge, they go in the Book, too. Your CFO (actually, her underlings—who have been making her look good for years now) prepares the financials and forecasts.

Don't get married to anything you write—because your advisors are going to take it all and "rewrite it" (think Edward Scissorhands). But they have to start somewhere. In the end, you'll be very pleased— it's all going to look brilliant. Some teams put the Book together, read it, and are so impressed with themselves that they don't want to sell their own company.

The Book will be 50 to 100 pages. Lots of charts. Pictures, too. In the old days, it would have been spiral bound (curly wire running through sheets of flattened wood called paper). Instead, you will scan it into a PDF and your investment banker will e-mail the Book to your prospects.

But be careful. Ahead lie bear traps in tall grass. One mistake with the Book and you'll sabotage your bargaining power or, worse, provide a guide to the destruction of your business.

## The Forecast Trap

The single biggest factor in how much you get for your company is your future earnings growth. You're the best source of this information, so the buyer needs you to make some predictions. How much are sales going to go up? What will happen to revenues each year? What will expenses look like? How much is going to drop to the bottom line? So buyers want—no, buyers demand—your predictions, which are called forecasts, or "pro formas."

Now we get to the tricky part. The rookie seller responds with optimism—wild optimism. He or she figures that there is nothing to lose by predicting incredible future sales. On the contrary, aren't I going to get more money if the buyer thinks my sales will skyrocket? Surely the deal will be done by the time the buyer sees if the forecasts were accurate. By then, what do I have to lose if my forecasts are wrong? A lot.

It's a trap. I call it the forecast trap.

Here's how one of the most boring tasks in the world turns into the nightmare of your life. Your financial advisors are helping you put together all the numbers that go in the Book. You'll need Operating Statements—showing your revenues and expenses for at least three, and sometimes five or more, prior years. You must also include Balance Sheets—showing your assets and liabilities—for at least the last two full years, plus your current, interim Balance Sheet. Then add data unique to your company—like particular metrics that drive your growth. For example, if you're an engineer and land sales are an early indicator of demand for your services, include a chart showing this key metric. Finally, you tackle the forecasts.

Most likely, you're selling for the first time. So you exaggerate future earnings. Again, no one will figure this out until it's too late, right? But the average buyer has done this before, plenty of times. They have made many painful mistakes in past deals. They know the "I'll goose up the numbers and they won't find out until it's too late" trick. They're not afraid. On the contrary, they're licking their chops.

You give them your "optimistic" forecast. First thing that wily buyer does is pin you down. They sit across the table, look you right in the eye, and ask how confident you are in your forecast. Trust me, you're going say you're certain—and the buyer knows that's what you'll say (it's part of the trap). Then the buyer will tighten the screws by pointing out that their purchase offer will be based on your forecast.

The trap is set. Now the deal s-l-o-w-s w-a-y d-o-w-n. The buyer said their due diligence would last one month, but it takes that long just to gather all of the information they want. Then you start the negotiation of the purchase agreement, also known as the second Hundred Years' War. The closing that was supposed to happen in three months doesn't. It doesn't happen after six months, either. The buyer always has more questions, or a hitch has come up with their financing, or suddenly they need to put out a fire at another company they bought. You're finally approaching a year since you gave your forecasts. Guess what? This is no accident.

The buyer can now compare your predictions to reality. If you were overly optimistic, they're going to slice you up. First, they question your management skills. Second, they take your sales price out to the chopping block and start whacking away: "We told you we were basing our offer on your forecasts, and now that the numbers are lower, we're not sure we want the company. But we certainly aren't paying the same amount."

Don't worry too much about them not wanting the company. That's unlikely—they wouldn't have spent this much time and effort if they didn't really want your business. But under these circumstances, I often see sellers get hammered with price reductions of 10 to 20 percent, and even as much as 40 percent in extreme cases.

Sure, if your results do match your wild predictions, all is well. The buyer is happy, and barring some other problem, you get all of your money. But you still took a big risk.

Here's what you should do. Aim a little low. Give the buyer a forecast that will be slightly less than what you believe will actually happen. Don't be too conservative, because that will take a big bite out of the sales price. Instead, provide a forecast that is 1 to 5 percent less than what you really think will happen. If you think that twelve months from now your sales will be $100 million, forecast sales of $95 million to $99 million. If you actually do a little better, it's all still good. Buyers like pleasant surprises.

When you forecast high and fall far short of your predictions, it's not pretty. Don't fall for the forecast trap.

Things could be worse. Some buyers aren't buyers at all. They just want to steal your ideas. So if you would be so kind as to sit down for a few months and write it all down, put it together in a book, and hand it to them . . .

## Steal This Book

Here's how it happens. A "buyer" pretends to be very interested in your business. Typically, they're going to come at you looking like a strategic buyer, not a financial one. They'll have a related business and they're looking to expand into yours. Or they're a competitor and they're looking to buy out the competition. But, of course, they need to examine the goods—closely—before they write a check.

One client was approached by one of these strategic buyers and red flags went up right away. We did a little homework and found out that the buyer's last "purchase" wasn't a purchase at all. In that con job, they'd gotten ahold of the seller's Book, studied it, and interviewed the seller's executives. Next thing, they manufactured an excuse to kill the deal. Within months they hired one of the seller's senior managers and started stealing the seller's customers away. They weren't buyers; they were thieves. We dug up the truth and refused to give them the

Book or even talk further. They slithered back under a rock somewhere—forked tongue up in the air sniffing for fresh prey.

This is business. You're going to learn one way or the other.

Here's the other way. Don't just hand out the Book like it's your résumé. Think of it more as a treasure map. Be careful. Make all prospective buyers sign a confidentiality agreement. But that's scant protection—like honor among thieves. Where there is a real competitive threat, you need to go further. You might need to prohibit them from hiring your employees for a year or more after you give them the Book. In extreme cases, you want them to agree they won't compete with you—at least for a while—if the deal dies. Realistically, most prospects won't agree to this. Their lawyers will tell them it will limit their options. Even if they're genuinely considering buying your business, they don't want to be locked out of your industry.

This is hard. Following these precautions takes discipline and judgment. You and your advisors will be afraid of scaring off purchasers with excessive demands. Sometimes it comes down to risking your company or risking a sale.

That's why you need to do your own due diligence about the buyers. Don't be bashful. They're checking you out. You need to examine them, too. If their story doesn't add up, you don't owe them anything—and definitely not your playbook.

A good Book tells your story. When it sells your business without running down the price or risking ruin, it's a bestseller.

# 27

# Dogs, Ponies, and the Deal Team

*Taking Your Show on the Road*

I t's the biggest deal of your life. You're finally selling your company. Everything has to be done just right, from making presentations about your company to negotiating the sale itself. But here's a shocker: you're about to jeopardize the sale and your company by putting your best people on the deal team.

It all starts when you finally decide to sell. You gather up everyone key to your business—your CFO, heads of sales and marketing, HR and IT chiefs, and general counsel. You call in your accounting and law firms and hire an investment banker. These all-stars, the guys and gals who are indispensable to your success, form your deal team.

The deal team pitches the sale of your company, negotiates deal terms, prepares the disclosure package, wades through the buyer's purchase agreement, and haggles and brawls it into shape. All of that talent—your best and brightest—single-mindedly focuses on one enormous, momentous task: selling your company.

Meanwhile your company falls apart.

You should have seen it coming. You robbed every major department in your company of their leaders. Then you put the remaining skeleton crew at the beck and call of the deal team—telling them to drop everything and jump to it when the deal team needed something. What did you expect?

## Don't Take Your Eye off the Ball

So who do you put on the deal team? Most entrepreneurs think that selling is so important, you have to put your most valuable people on the deal team.

How does that work, again? You put your top salesperson, your best financial person, your super thinkers and doers on the deal team. Now jump to the thick of the negotiations and due diligence.

While the investment bankers, lawyers, and accountants are working on deal terms and contract language, the rest of the deal team responds to the buyers' lists of questions and document requests. These lists are miles long. Your team is working day and night to gather data, draft answers, prepare spreadsheets, assemble documents, and retrieve information. They're on hours-long phone conferences with the buyer's due-diligence teams answering follow-up questions. They're giving guided tours of your facilities to buyers and their investors and lenders. They're traveling to the buyers' home offices for following up meetings. It's all coming together, right? Not so much.

No one's minding the store. Your top salesperson hasn't talked to a customer in three months. Her team is scared, whining, and floundering. Sales are suffering. Down the hall, your financial guy hasn't prepared mandatory reports for your banks. Your lenders are getting nervous. Downstairs, your HR chief is busy responding to tasks from the buyer, like checking on which employees have noncompete agreements, providing details on benefit plans, and giving histories of disputes with ex-employees. Morale has cratered because employees know big changes are coming but not where they fit in. They're either depressed or surfing Monster.com for new jobs.

You don't even know what's going on with your company. All your major new initiatives and half of your regular projects have been neglected. None of your rank-and-file employees are getting any answers or support. Your competitors are beating you out on new contract awards.

Revenues dip. Profits slide. Good people leave the company.

Suddenly the buyer is alarmed. They're not even sure they want the company anymore. Certainly they want to pay less. But worse, they're seriously questioning whether you can chew gum and run a business at the same time.

What the heck happened here?

You took your eye off the ball.

## The Right Stuff

How do you avoid this kind of fiasco? Contrary to what you'll hear from almost everyone else, the people on your deal team should not be folks who are critical to your day-to-day operations. Selling your business usually takes anywhere from six months to a year. You can't drag away the folks who are indispensable to running the company and put them on the deal team.

Take your finance department, for example. Given the stakes, it's better to have your outside CPA preparing financial info for the buyer than it is to drag your CFO away from her duties and decapitate part of your business. You can't run your company without financial information, you can't maintain banking relationships without an accessible CFO, and you can't grow without constant input from your CFO. How could you have her—or any other key employee, for that matter—take on a second full-time job and expect the company to thrive, much less survive?

One client put key people on his deal team—over my objections—and refused to hire enough outside consultants. He thought it was too expensive. But after a couple of months, his team was stretched thin and his company started to fall apart. Still he wouldn't get the help he needed. Instead he stopped responding to the buyers' requests and tried to stampede his way through the final negotiations and close the deal. But that produced the opposite reaction. The buyers got scared and froze the deal in its tracks—they thought were dealing with a whack-job. We talked the buyers down from the ledge, acted as an intermediary to get them needed info, and closed out the deal without taking too much of a haircut on the price. But the seller didn't maximize the deal—he left millions on the table because he wouldn't spend a few hundred grand on a couple of key consultants.

For this client and a lot of sellers, the right deal team is a mixture of consultants and employees. In a company with a strong finance department, your CFO may be able to join the deal team because there are a couple of able lieutenants to keep the department thriving. In another situation, one or more outside CPAs will have to join the team, work closely with your employees to get up to speed, and then respond to buyer requests. Depending on the nature of your business, you will want senior people, but not department chiefs, on the deal team. A Vice President in your technology department may be able to serve as an able conduit between your Chief Technology Officer and your buyer, without pulling your CTO away from vital tasks. Of course, in addition to your outside accounting firm, you should also expect to involve and lean heavily on your investment bankers and outside lawyers. These are some of the final costs of doing business in order to sell your business.

But it is not enough just to open your wallet or keep essential personnel at their desks. To attract buyers in the first place, you need to select members of the deal team to put on a show.

## The Dog and Pony Shows

When you start the selling process, you write the Book on your company—everything a buyer would want to know about your business. Then you create a list of prospective buyers and start pitching your company. The buyers who are interested get the Book—after they sign nondisclosure and other agreements. If the Book does its job, you're going on the road. You'll make dozens of presentations—called dog and pony shows—to prospective buyers.

At this point, the typical buyer is interested but not sold. They've read the Book and asked around about your company. They think that they might be able to make money by buying it. But they have a lot of questions. In fact, a typical buyer will usually send two or three people—maybe more—to the dog and pony show. At least one of them is on a mission to ask tough questions that stump you. So you need to put as much effort into these presentations as you do into any other part of selling your company.

## Show and Sell

The dog and pony shows are a job interview, class presentation, and Cirque du Soleil all wrapped up in one—and much more important.

**PICK YOUR PRESENTERS CAREFULLY:** Your presenters need to know a lot about the company. But even more, they need to present well. You may even want to bring someone from your company who is not part of the deal team but adds some sizzle to the show, like one of your top salespeople. That brilliant guy who works for you and solves incredible problems but says the strangest, stupidest things? He's not in the show.

**PRACTICE:** Tell the "yes-men" on your team to take a break, and round up your toughest critics for some practice sesssions. Have them ask the hard questions. Figure out how you're going to answer the tough questions. Do it now, before you're in the middle of a presentation. Take it from someone who's been there: it's excruciating when one guy on your team leans over to another—in front of the buyers—and asks, "What's our answer to that question?" Awkward!

**DRY RUN WITH "BAD DATES":** Do at least two or three real presentations for buyers you don't care about before you present to your top prospects. Despite all of the practice, you'll encounter questions you didn't anticipate and you'll polish rough spots in your presentation. It's like starting in Topeka before you face the big Broadway crowds and critics.

**JUST THE FACTS, PLEASE:** At the presentation, start with an overview of the company, summarizing the same information you provided in the Book. Keep it short—fifteen to thirty minutes, tops. The buyers are here to ask questions.

**DON'T BE POLITICIANS:** Answer the damn questions. These buyers are very smart people. They can tell the difference between an answer and evasion. They'd rather hear an admission about your weaknesses than fear you don't understand the problem or haven't come to grips with it. Every company has problems. Winners deal with them.

**CURTAIN CALL:** Give them a show that says you've got a great business that will make them a lot of money. When the shows are over, you want at least three, and preferably more, buyers that are dying to buy your company.

Building a great company is not enough. To sell it, you need the right cast on the stage and behind the scenes. Both the show and the business must go on.

# 28

# The Best Way to Sell Your Company

*The Art of Creating an Auction*

Lightning struck. You just put your business up for sale and got an offer of $50 million. That's a lot of money. More than you ever dreamed. Your advisors are screaming, "Take it; take it!" and making stupid cash register sounds—"cha-ching, cha-ching." Your spouse thinks you're crazy for not jumping at the offer ("the things that we could do with all that money"). Confidants are taking you aside, with dead serious looks on their faces, and telling you this kind of opportunity doesn't come along every day. How could this be bad?

It's not bad; it's worse. This is like some game show drama come to life. Your business could be worth more—a lot more—but this offer comes with an ultimatum. Accept immediately or they walk away forever. Take the money in the briefcase. Or take your chances.

You can't stall—they won't wait. But you can't accept their offer and still be comfortable you got the best price. And you can't turn it down and risk a much worse outcome. It's a good problem to have, but it's still a problem. There's only one good solution: don't let this happen to you in the first place.

Getting top dollar—and knowing it—takes timing, patience, and discipline.

It takes an auction.

## Get Them Fighting over You

Why conduct an auction? Because an auction gets you more money for your company. An auction is a competition among buyers to purchase your business. Buyers pay more when they compete. For one thing, most buyers are never really certain how much a company is worth. When others are willing to pay even more, it confirms the buyer's valuation of your company. Auctions also stimulate competition. Go to any auction and you find plenty of people who get caught up in the drive to "win" the auction and spend more than they planned.

But an auction doesn't just happen. You won't find buyers spontaneously lined up outside your door, offers in hand. You have to draw up and execute a careful, custom-tailored plan.

## The Plan

Here is the formula for creating an auction:

**TIMING:** You have to wait until you and the market are ready. If you try to sell too soon, before you've perfected your business, you present too much risk—risk of losses (versus profits) and risk of failure. Buyers will be scared and offer less or won't bid at all. Likewise, you don't want to sell at a bad time for your industry. But if there is demand for companies like yours, the price rockets up. You should start monitoring the market and talking to investment bankers two to three years before you think you're ready to sell.

If you have to pick between your company and your industry being ready, sell when your industry is hot. Buyers will overlook issues and pay crazy prices when they are dying to get into your field. Better to have a lot of a fool's money than half as much from a wise person.

**PATIENCE:** Don't marry the first guy with a ring. Make it clear when you hire your investment banker and other advisors that you're not falling into bed with the first buyer who winks at you. Don't allow anyone on your team who doesn't share that restraint. Some advisors are lazy or nervous. They want you to run off and elope with the first buyer who shows some interest.

**DISCIPLINE:** Market your company in a disciplined fashion. Create a schedule for the marketing of your company, including the following:

- Do your initial pitches and send the Book.

- Solicit offers—simultaneously—from all prospective buyers. Include an identical deadline for submission of the buyers' offers. This helps you manage that early offer with a "take-it-or-leave-it" ultimatum.

- Don't respond piecemeal to individual offers. Again, you're trying to keep multiple options open.

- Review the offers and trim your list—if you have that luxury. Ask the top three to five buyers for their best and final offers. Give them some guidance on where they need to improve their terms.

- Negotiate—again, simultaneously—with your top three candidates. Some advisors say stop here and work only with one. The problem is if you stop too soon and hook up with just one buyer, then you lose the competitive pressure that produces the best deal.

- Keep as many buyers involved as long as you can. Once you have picked one buyer, the others will move on to other deals. When that happens, you lose bargaining power. So you want to nail down the best deal you can get, before you lose the advantage.

## Warning: Hidden Agendas

One of your advisors may have an affinity for a particular buyer and try to coerce you into dealing with them. They may be doing a lot of business with that buyer or expect some kind of payback for the shotgun wedding. So they'll grease the skids for that buyer and in the process cripple the auction. That's where the discipline in your plan is so critical. Stick with simultaneous everything—submission of the Book, receipt of offers, responses, requests for best and final offers, and negotiations. Everyone who is interested in your company gets to play on a level field. No one gets an early peek or the chance to tempt you into ignoring other offers. It takes more work and a heck of a lot of leadership to keep everyone in line. But it pays.

Still there won't be any bidding war if there isn't a lot of demand for your business.

## An Honest Assessment

How do you know if you'll be in demand? Well, first, don't get fooled by the praise of your colleagues. That's like your mother saying you did well in the school play. What else is she going to say?

Here are some surefire signs of demand:

- Companies have already made unsolicited offers to invest in or buy your business.

- Your industry is considered the wave of the future and is frequently featured in the news.

- It is easy for you to borrow money from banks and other commercial lenders.

- Your employees take less pay than they could get elsewhere in exchange for stock options, warrants, or other interests in your company.

- You're winning awards, your products are hot, and there is buzz about your business.

If you don't recognize any of these signs, you can still sell your company. Just because you're not going to the Moon doesn't mean you're not going for a ride. Plenty of companies sell for a lot of bucks without multiple offers or an auction. Think arranged marriage versus coming out at a debutante ball.

But without a lot of demand for your company, you don't want to be too aggressive. You don't want to insist on an auction and turn off the one or two people who are interested in buying your company. You need that honest assessment first. If there is a lot of demand, go for the auction. If not, work with your advisors and start negotiating with the best candidate to buy your company. Business success is all too often like a casino. One moment you're ahead and the next you're behind. There are a lot worse things that you can do than take your chips off the table when you're up.

Realistically, there is a much greater chance that only one or two buyers will be really motivated to purchase your business. Widespread demand is pretty rare. Spend the time to determine where you stand. But if the buyers are out there beating down your door, don't miss the opportunity. Create an auction. Let the bidding begin.

# 29

## Strengthening Your Bargaining Power

*Boosting Your Leverage*

Here's part of my standard sermon for sellers. "Even if you've decided to sell, you've still got to run your business like you're not," I implore them. "Until you actually sell, don't ease up. If you relax, bad stuff happens. Business will suffer, the buyer will find out, and that jeopardizes your payday. You'll get less—maybe nothing."

But there are nonbelievers. Here's what happens to "ye of little faith":

- A seller didn't refinance his business loan. I mean, why pay the closing costs and legal fees for a refi when the buyer promised to close in three months? Then the buyer "got delayed" and there the seller was, six months later, with the loan coming due and still no sales proceeds to pay it off. On the verge of defaulting on the ballooning loan, the seller caved, took a big hit on the price, and sold in desperation.

- One seller stopped bidding on new contracts, thinking it was too time-consuming and expensive and wouldn't pay off before closing. Shocker alert! When the deal got delayed, the pipeline of new sales shriveled. Guess what else shrunk? The price for the business.

- Another seller cut his advertising budget and thought he was fooling everyone when he pocketed the savings. The dip in sales wouldn't show up for a while and the price for the business was already set in stone—sandstone, it turns out, very fragile sandstone.

In a basketball game, never take a lead for granted. Play hard till the final buzzer. In a sprint, don't run to the finish line. Race through it. Same goes with selling your business. Never ease up or need to sell. Run it like you're never selling.

When you don't need to sell, you can tell buyers to take it or leave it. One client, Danny, did just that. Buyers were crawling all over his company and he acted like selling was the last thing on his mind. He ran his business like he was never selling. Danny's indifference actually attracted buyers. These buyers were used to seeing flawed businesses and sellers who were eager to unload. The opposite situation—a well-run company and a confident owner—drove the buyers into a frenzy. They were practically throwing offers at Danny. But Danny told the buyers he was only selling if the deal was quick, pricey, and "as is." Some buyers dropped out of the running, but the rest competed to buy the business.

Danny's case was an extreme example of how to boost leverage. Few entrepreneurs can hide their desire to sell or run their businesses as if they're keeping them forever. But this is the gospel truth: never need to sell your business. Run it like you're never going to.

You'll get a better deal.

Can I get an "Amen"?

# 30

# The Letter of Intent

## Picking a Winning Battleground

Wise warriors seek battlefields that give them the advantage. Everyone from military strategists to athletes understands the power of a playing field tilted in their favor. In sports, raucous crowds—the "12th Man"—drown out the visiting team's play calling. In politics, the home field advantage is so strong, they call the beneficiary a Native Son. Since the earliest wars, armies have sought high ground and terrain that aided victory. A battlefield that gives you an inherent edge can be critical to winning.

But you're never going to win if you don't realize you've just stepped onto a battlefield. Clever buyers know the first—often crucial—battleground is the letter of intent. In the LOI, the purchaser sets out the terms of their offer—how much they will pay, when, and what you have to do to earn it.

Sellers often look at the LOI like it is a Hallmark greeting card or a love letter. ("They like me. They really like me.") But there is something else going on here, sometimes far more consequential and often sinister. Despite appearances, this is not just a simple list of business terms. The LOI is the first battle. Victory here gives the buyer a vantage point to rain boulders down on you throughout the rest of the negotiations.

## Unilateral Disarmament

As audacious as it sounds, the first thing buyers want you to do in the LOI is give up your bargaining power. Virtually every buyer is going to demand that you deal with their group exclusively. They'll argue that they're going to devote a lot of time and money negotiating with you, so it's only fair that you work only with them. There is a lot of truth in this argument. But taken to extremes both this and other buyer demands will reduce you to a punching bag.

What are the extremes?

- Some buyers want an exclusive negotiating period that goes on for months and months. During this time period, other interested buyers will move on to other deals. You'll be losing the very suitors who are most interested in you. So limit the exclusivity period to no more than ninety days. You can always extend the exclusivity period if the buyer is playing nice. Also, try to put milestones in the LOI. After you agree to the LOI, the next two steps are negotiation of the purchase agreement and the buyer's due diligence regarding your company. Some buyers drag out this process, hoping to weaken your resolve. Push back. If the buyer doesn't deliver their proposed purchase agreement to you within thirty or forty-five days, you should be allowed to negotiate with others. If you are dealing with a buyer exclusively, you need to keep their feet to the fire.

- The overreaching buyer doesn't just want you to be exclusive; they want you to report anyone who makes a pass at you. Some proposed LOIs require that you reveal any competing offer you receive from another party during the exclusivity period. The buyer wants to know what other people are willing to pay and—if it's lower—use it against you. Agreeing to that arrangement is like working for the enemy. You're not married yet. You're not even engaged. You're just dating. Strike that provision.

- Let's go from the ridiculous to the absurd. The buyer wants *you* to pay *their* legal fees if the deal doesn't happen. Huh? I know; it's crazy. That's what I said when I first heard it. Here's how it works. You sign the LOI and then, sooner or later (mostly later), they send you an outrageously one-sided purchase agreement. It has all kinds of vile provisions. But the more you fight back, the bigger their/your legal bill. If you kill the deal, you have to pay it. It's like quicksand. The more you struggle, the more you sink. Don't agree to that one.

## Ruling Things Out

Believe it or not, it gets worse. It's not enough for the LOI to spell out the terms of the deal. You have to say what's *n-o-t* part of the deal. Strange as it sounds, plenty of buyers feel it is fair game to put just about anything in the purchase agreement if you don't explicitly rule it out in the LOI.

This is where your advisors are invaluable. You likely can't imagine all of the horrors that are out there. For example, the LOI says you'll get an IOU for part of the purchase price. What the LOI doesn't say is that the buyer plans to mortgage the hell out of your business and strip it of every penny of equity. Just like dead-broke home owners who mail their keys to the bank, if business goes bad the buyer is going to walk away from that note you're holding. If you don't prohibit, or at least cap, how much the buyer can borrow, then you leave yourself exposed to the risk of not getting paid.

You wouldn't think you have to tell the purchaser not to punch you in the face. But history shows it's not a bad idea to get it in writing.

## Unintended Consequences

Some buyers are smart, smart, smart. They're so sharp that one day you're feeling fat and happy signing an LOI that's going to make you rich and the next day you're standing in the parking lot outside your former business with your pockets turned inside out, scratching your head trying to figure out where all of the money went.

Here are two classics from the purchaser trick bag:

1. The LOI provides that the buyer is purchasing your company lock, stock, and barrel. They get everything—which you don't realize includes your cash. Then, in a separate provision, they require that you run the company "in the ordinary course of business." This clause expressly prohibits any bonuses, dividends, or other distributions. The purchaser convinces you that it wouldn't be right for you to strip value out of the business by paying out extra money. But if your business does well, cash builds up in your kitty. Lots of cash. This next part is brilliant and sad, all in one. When they buy your business, they get your cash! In effect, they get to use that money—your money—to pay you for your business. Sort of makes you feel like a stupid hooker—giving away your booty for free.

   Even if you are selling everything, you can still exclude cash or, at the very least (and we do this often), cap the amount you have to turn over. This actually reverses the trick, because as time goes by, you get to pocket more and more cash.

2. In the LOI, purchasers try to structure their offer so that it is based on a formula, but the price is capped. If the business does great, you don't get any more money. But if your revenue or profit goes down, they apply the formula and you get less.

It's the old heads you lose, tails they win. Instead, either fix the price so that it can't go up *or* down or forget the fixed price and use a formula that lets the price go up, as well as down.

The negotiation of the LOI is the first battle and the terms of the LOI establish the battlefield for all future negotiations. Buyers know this. They come equipped with every trick of the trade and try to create permanent home field advantage. The savvy buyer wants you to throw down your weapons and be forced into unconditional surrender.

Instead, negotiate the details now and preempt problems. Don't fall for their trick formulas. They'll make a deal sound good now but turn out much worse later. Don't rush through the LOI. Pick it apart. You'll reap rich rewards if you get the LOI right.

Certainly there will be fights to come. But if you're careful at the outset, you'll hold on to your bargaining power.

Don't disarm. Fight back.

# 31

# The Deal

*What's in It for You?*

Some sellers want a pile of cash. They dream about buying an island or a house on every continent.

Others want stock in the buyer, so that they can become part of something larger and maybe catch a ride on the next big thing.

Some just want a job and a steady paycheck. They fantasize about someone else doing all of the worrying. They'd prefer to keep their heads down, work hard, and sleep well at night.

You've busted your hump for years. You were smart and lucky. You persevered. It all came together. People want to buy your company. It's not Genie-in-the-Bottle-with-Three-Wishes time, but you're still facing a big decision. You need to think hard and get it right.

What's in it for you?

## What's Behind Door Number Three?

You only get to sell your company once. The buyer is going to want plenty from you. What do you want in exchange for your company? First, let's start with the menu. Here are the classic choices:

**CASH:** This one is good. If they're offering cash, take it.

**PROMISSORY NOTE:** This one is usually bad. Many buyers will offer you an IOU for some or all of the purchase price for your company. Usually you get paid in monthly installments or in a lump sum—or some combination of both. In reality, if your former company isn't making money, you might not get paid at all. So if you get an IOU, technically a "promissory note," you need to nail down a lot of things. For starters, who gets paid before you? Can the buyer issue dividends and bonuses but not pay you? Can the folks who buy your company go on a shopping spree, run out of money, and then stiff you? Is there any collateral you can grab if they don't pay you? The questions go on and on, and your lawyers need to protect you.

Why even take a promissory note? Well, sometimes it's that or nothing.

**EARN-OUT:** This one is tricky. An "earn-out" is money you get later if your old company does well after you sell it. Unless they've kept you on to run the show, you're taking a big chance that the purchasers know what they're doing, will run the business well, and will hit the targets required for your earn-out payment. What if the buyer owns several companies and neglects yours? What if the buyer owns several companies and steers sales—which could have gone to your old company—to another business? To some people, *not* paying you is just as good as making money.

Ordinarily the buyer has the motivation to try to make a success of your old business. Presumably they gave you a big down payment and the earn-out is just a bonus. But if the down payment is small and the earn-out large, the buyer has less at stake and you're taking a big chance. First, try to get more cash up front. If that doesn't work, do your own due diligence. See what the buyer has done with past acquisitions. If you don't find any horror stories, have your lawyers add a half-dozen pages of protections to the purchase agreement and hope for the best.

Some earn-outs offer real upside. You have the chance to make a lot more money if your company does well after the sale. Mostly, though, you take an earn-out—like a promissory note—because you've got no choice.

**EMPLOYMENT:** This one cuts both ways. On the one hand, some buyers want to make sure you're going to stay on, mind the store, and protect their investment. They're afraid things will fall apart if you leave. On the other hand, some sellers actually want to stay on and get a job with good pay and benefits as part of the deal.

If they want you and you'd rather move on, limit how long you're going to be an indentured servant. One year might not be enough for the buyer, and more than three years is likely too much for you. If you're concerned—and even if you're not— obtain the following protections:

- A *nailed down pecking order.* Typically, you'll only want to report to the President (if that's not you) or the CEO (if you are the President).

- *Limited duties.* You don't want to be emptying wastebaskets just because someone wants to mess with you.

- *Identification of where you're going to work,* and don't let them move it more than a certain number of miles—ten or twenty in a big city, fifty in a more rural area.

- *Limitations on buyer's remedies* if you breach the agreement and walk away from the job. Don't let them take back the purchase price—at worst, keep it to a small slice of the price.

- *Prohibition of salary reductions.* Don't just spell out your salary, or you could get caught up in across-the-board cuts or they could single you out. Also, require that your benefits are as good as those of the other senior company executives.

If you want the job—that is, if the job is part of what's bargained for—also do the following:

- Don't let them fire you without a good reason—called "for cause" in legal jargon.

- Get the right to terminate your employment and still get paid your salary and perks if the buyer materially breaches the agreement. In lawyer-speak this is a "good reason" termination. You're making sure they can't jerk you around so you'll quit with nothing.

- Make sure the buyer can't resell your company without either paying you off or obligating the new buyer to keep you on.

**STOCK:** You may have the opportunity—or the obligation—to take part of the purchase price in stock. Depending on the structure of the deal, this could be stock in your company or in the buying entity. Either way, you have a whole host of issues to grapple with:

- If you are counting on having a certain percentage of the stock, can your share be diluted? Or do you have the right to purchase more stock on the same terms that it is offered to anyone else so that you maintain your desired percentage of the company ("preemptive" rights)?

- If the rest of the shareholders make a deal to sell their stock, can you insist on getting cut into the deal ("tag-along" rights)? Or can they insist that you sell along with them ("drag-along" rights)?

- If the other shareholders register their stock to sell it publicly, will yours be registered, too ("piggyback" rights)?

Bigger still, you're facing the fundamental question of getting out of the business or staying in. Usually, you're going to lose control of your business. You may keep a bit of power over how things are run. You may even negotiate a veto over certain decisions, but that is rare. Unquestionably, you're taking an economic risk. Whether you're keeping some stock in your old company or getting paid with stock in a new company, you're essentially making a bet. Are you willing to give up cash for whatever is behind Door Number Three?

There is no easy way to predict the outcome.

## Doubling Down or Cashing Out

One client sold his government contracting business for $30-plus million—all cash. After he split the money with his partners, he still had plenty left. Then he turned around and invested the loot in that sucker punch called a diversified portfolio. He's going back to work now.

Another guy, the uncle of a friend, ran the most boring business on Earth. It sold zip code guides—back when people cared about such things. Strangely enough, someone wanted to buy the company. The owner sold the business for a decent amount of cash—nothing to retire on. But he was forced to take some of the purchase price in stock in the buyer's company. A few years later the buyer was acquired and the uncle's stock was exchanged for new shares of a bigger company. Then it happened again and he really struck it rich. This time he traded his shares for a pile of very valuable stock in a big publicly traded company. He sold the stock decades ago and it made him rich. He still is.

So while cash sounds good, it's not a sure thing. There are plenty of times when people have let their payoff ride in company stock and it grew.

## The Wrinkles (AKA You Can't Be Too Paranoid)

You're going to hit the big points of the deal in the LOI—like the sales price and how it is paid. Your team will hammer out the fine points in the deal documents—like the terms of promissory notes, employment agreement, and stock rights. But there are wrinkles.

Remember your Payday plan? To motivate your employees and help get to this fortuitous event, you established a stock option plan and gave out thousands of stock options. Everybody's happy now—or at least they should be. But you still need to be careful and protect against the "what-ifs." Like what if you accept employment with the new buyer and one of your devoted employees accuses you of diverting money from the group Payday to your own pocket via a fat paycheck? What if one of your trusted VPs sues you for not getting enough money for the company because you didn't shop it adequately? Yes, these things really happen. In fact, selling CEOs increasingly hire financial consultants to evaluate the sale and render "fairness opinions" to ward off these very lawsuits. Here you are getting ready to throw the biggest party in company history and you still have to make sure you're not going to end up doing a perp walk.

There's more. There are lockup periods that limit your ability to sell any stock you receive. You might have to wait a year to sell the stock. Meanwhile the price dives. Or consider this wrinkle: the buyer agrees to a purchase price and then tries to shave it down. Buried in the deal documents is a provision making you pay the accrued vacation pay for all of your former employees. You end up with an unexpected six-figure obligation.

The bigger the sales price, the more there is to worry about. If you're not careful, "what's in it for you" is whole lot less than you were expecting.

No one said it was going to be easy.

# 32

# Tax Consequences

## *The Deal* Within *the Deal*

Here's a rookie mistake: wait to worry about taxes until you're ready to close on the sale—when it's too late to do anything about it. Buyers don't do that—they know a battle when they see one coming. They strategize about taxes before the first handshake. They understand that the purchase price is only part of the deal. What matters is what you net—the amount you put in your pocket. A word or two in the right contract clause cuts their taxes in half and doubles yours. You need to fight back with tax smarts or lose the deal within the deal.

### Tug-of-War

When it comes to taxes on the sale of your business, you are in a zero-sum game—not a win-win situation. The more tax you pay, the less the buyer pays.

Think of it like a tug-of-war. If you pull the rope toward yourself, you are dragging someone else along the ground. The difference between doing the pulling and getting dragged really matters. If you dodge a tax, they pay one. When you pay a big tax bill, they get a great write-off.

For example, if the buyer lowers the purchase price by a million dollars and instead gives you a job for five years at $200,000 per year, you're going to pay a lot more taxes. Salary is taxed at a much higher rate than your capital gain on the sale. Meanwhile, the buyer gets a much bigger write-off for your compensation than they would for the higher price.

Your tax bill easily doubles if buyers get their way. Win-lose, not win-win.

## Big Issues

In any deal, there may be two or three issues that could double your tax bill and ruin the deal for you. Often the biggest issue is whether the buyer is purchasing your assets or your stock. The taxes can range from 20 to over 50 percent of the sales price depending on the structure of your deal:

**STOCK SALE:** If you sell your stock (or other equity interests, such as membership interests in an LLC), then you're usually going to get taxed at capital gains rates. That's good. These are the lowest tax rates—usually about 20 percent of the sales price depending on what Congress and your state legislature had for breakfast.

**ASSET SALE:** Your tax bill could easily double if you sell your assets. For instance, if someone bought your moving company in an asset sale, you would be selling your trucks, warehouse, trademarks, and customer list, instead of the stock in your company. With this kind of deal, it is not unusual that some assets are subject to "recapture" at ordinary income tax rates ranging to 40 percent. That's bad.

**STUPID SALE:** Heaven forbid if you have a regular "C" corporation and you sell your assets. You'll get taxed twice and get the worst result of all. Your corporation will get taxed on the sale of the assets, and then you'll get taxed again on the distribution of the profits. You'll pay more than 50 percent of the price in taxes! Not a brilliant move. Only bad planning and a predatory buyer could produce such a disaster.

## Little Issues

Even when you're not dealing with issues that can multiply your tax bill, there is plenty to plan for:

**TIMING:** If you close early next year, instead of late this year, you can put off paying your tax bill on the sale for an extra year. If your tax bill is millions of dollars, there is a lot of value in a year's free use of this money—like earning interest on FDIC-insured CDs.

**PHANTOM INCOME:** Make sure you get enough money in the sale to pay your tax bill. Sometimes you don't get cash but something else of value. Uncle Sam doesn't care. He still wants his cut. Even if you only got some magic beans for the sale of your cow, you've still got a tax bill to pay.

**ALLOCATIONS:** When you sell assets—instead of stock—the IRS makes you allocate the purchase price among the various assets you sell. You might pay 15 percent on the sale of one asset and double that on the sale of another. For instance, if you sell your furniture store, your inventory might be taxed at one rate, the building at another rate, and your customer list at a still different rate. So these allocations can make a big difference in your tax bill. While there are rules for these allocations, there may be gray areas. Consult with your tax experts. Depending on how you allocate the price, your tax bill will grow or shrink.

None of this is a cakewalk. And remember, what helps you hurts the buyer.

## One Constant: Nothing Stays the Same

As I am writing this, Congress is passing a major new tax law (I get to put that line in everything I write). There's no particular logic in it. They wake up on the wrong side of the bed, they're cranky, and they just feel like it. By the time you read this, I'm sure they've changed it again.

Tax laws are constantly morphing. You can't count on last year's laws applying next year. Sometimes you can't even count on last month's rules. Often famous laws are chiseled into marble buildings. You never see that with tax laws.

Arm yourself early with the tax consequences of a sale. Your opponents surely will. They thrive on playing all the angles. So before you ever begin negotiating a deal, know the law, what to ask for, and what you're really going to get. Then surround yourself with experts and stay on your toes. The rules could shift beneath your feet.

What you pay in taxes is as important as what the buyer pays you. It's the deal within the deal.

# 33

## Post-Sale Terms

### *The Deal* After *the Deal*

L ike so many entrepreneurs, Bart ran out of money on the way to world domination. He had struggled to build the first national chain of bicycle stores. But cash was so tight he couldn't grow the business. That forced him to take on investors. It wasn't exactly a marriage made in heaven. After a year butting heads, Bart gladly sold out. Business was no better for the investors. In just a few years, they put the company in bankruptcy, fired their employees, and abandoned their leases.

That's when Bart got The Call.

Many people get The Call. The folks who invested with Bernie Madoff—they got The Call. The guys who worked their whole career at a once successful, now defunct company, and retired on big fat pensions—they got The Call. When the investors bankrupted Bart's old business, the landlord for one of the bike stores pulled out an old lease with Bart's signature on it and gave him The Call.

It turns out that a long time ago Bart had personally guaranteed one of his store leases. He put everything he owned—which at the time wasn't much—on the line because in the early days that was the only way to lease the space. Now the landlord was demanding hundreds of thousands of dollars in unpaid rent from Bart. After all this time, after he had sold his interest, after he had nothing at all to do with the business for years, how could he possibly still be on the hook for a six-figure company obligation? Bart was flabbergasted.

"How? How? How?" That's what Bart kept asking himself as he lay in bed each night, his stomach churning. He even called the company lawyers and yelled at them. It turns out they were never his lawyers—they worked for the investors. When he sold the investors a majority interest in the business, the investors brought in their own lawyers. They weren't paid to look out for Bart's interests and they hadn't.

The simple answer is that Bart signed a guarantee with no expiration date. When he sold the business, no one tore up the guarantee or made the investors take it over. Ironically, after all the sweat and tears trying to build the business, the only thing about his company that lasted was that damn guarantee. And it wasn't like he had made a bundle on the sale. So the landlord's call hit Bart like a punch in the gut.

That's how Bart learned a painful lesson about the deal after the deal.

In Bart's case and so many others, people aren't careful. They get zapped by an old agreement they didn't terminate or a new one they don't think through. These things don't happen every day, but they're more common than lightning strikes—and just as painful. There are all kinds of loose ends that can trip you up if you're not careful.

## Loose Ends

When you sell, you need to take an inventory of all the things that could come back to haunt you. First, consider all of the old stuff. Did you sign any personal guarantees like Bart? Did one of your employees spill chemicals down the floor drain in your warehouse? Did someone slip in the parking lot of your office complex? Is some big company alleging that you violated their patent? The question is whether there are any lawsuits out there waiting to happen. Think hard. Ask around. Make a list.

If you have any of these skeletons in your closet, don't ignore them. Now is your best and last chance to tackle these problems and clean the slate. Once you sell, you lose all leverage. Take action:

**RELEASES:** Figure out where you're still personally liable and make the selling and buying teams get you off the hook. In Bart's case, he should have asked the buyer to offer up a new guarantee of the store lease so the landlord would tear up his.

**INDEMNIFICATION:** Get the buyer to agree that they will take care of any future lawsuits against you. Of course, this requires that you spell out who might sue you and why. The buyer needs that info to weigh the risk. You may have to make some concessions to get this protection—even lower the sales price. But you need to put the risks on the table and find out what it will cost to get protection. Otherwise, you'll end up just sitting there by the phone, hoping no one calls.

**INSURANCE:** Sometimes you or the buyer needs to purchase an insurance policy to get the right protection. If you or your company might be responsible for a spill of hazardous materials and you're concerned that the seller doesn't have deep enough pockets to fend off any lawsuits and pay any claims, you need a solid insurance company in the background, standing ready to bail you out of trouble.

With the right protections, you'll get some peace of mind. But it's not all just about keeping the past in the past.

When you sell your business, you're going to enter into a bunch of new agreements, many of which could come back to haunt you. The list of potential traps is long and includes the following:

**NONCOMPETE AGREEMENTS:** Almost always, you have to agree that you won't work for a competitor for at least a few months or years after the sale. Make sure that you can work for a business that doesn't really compete with your old one. The noncompete agreement shouldn't define any entrepreneur with a pulse as a "competitor." Limit the time period of your noncompete restriction. Finally, the whole agreement should evaporate if the buyer goes under or stops paying money they owe you.

**NONSOLICITATION AGREEMENTS:** Similarly, the buyer often makes you agree that you won't poach your old employees—at least for a while. If you have a favorite colleague whom you do want to take into some brave new world, bargain for an exception now—again, while you have some leverage. Also, try to get the right to hire any employee who gets RIFed by the buyer after you leave.

**INDEMNIFICATION AGREEMENTS:** Here's where you agree to protect the buyer if someone claims you did something bad while you were running the company. Try to keep this to a minimum. It's fair to bail out the buyer if you committed fraud or didn't pay your taxes. But don't put yourself on the hook for run-of- the-mill stuff, like bad deals or things you already disclosed—especially if the buyer already used those things to negotiate a lower price.

**INTELLECTUAL PROPERTY AGREEMENTS:** If your business is involved in any kind of software, technology, or other creations, feel free to transfer it all to the buyer. But be careful about promises that you were the sole creator of all of this intellectual property. Your company may very well have worked with consultants who still have rights to use these works. Or you may have unknowingly duplicated the very same thing that someone else already made. Also, if you invented something in your spare time that had nothing to do with the company, make sure to carve that out and keep it.

**CONFIDENTIALITY AGREEMENTS:** The buyer wants you to keep your mouth shut after you sell. Make sure that they at least let you breathe. These agreements can really go overboard—like forbidding you from telling your accountant how much you made last year. You should always be able to talk to your professional advisors. Also, tweak the agreement so the buyer is only protecting important stuff, not every scrap of info that ever passed in front of your eyes.

You don't want to be paranoid and imagine only the worst. But don't act reckless and ignore the risks.

## Take Off Those Rose-Colored Glasses

Think with your head, not your heart. Plan; don't dream. So many horror stories could have been avoided with just a bit of care. That old saying about an ounce of prevention being worth a pound of cure is so true when you sell your business.

You can't just hope everything is going to take care of itself. Consider the possibilities and protect against them.

## The Checklist

1. Don't assume that someone is protecting you. Bart did— and look at what happened to him. The buyer's people most certainly are not. Nail down who has your back.

2. Develop a list of all of things that could possibly lead to any future exposure. This ranges from the assistant who threatened you with a harassment suit, to the contracts your company may have breached, to any laws that may have been broken. Certainly include anything you ever personally guaranteed.

3. Get advice on which risks to worry about. Some aren't really a problem at all. Others require a lot of attention.

4. Negotiate protections, ranging from releases from old agreements, to indemnification by the buyer, to insurance policies.

## . . . And One for All

Finally, watch out for a phenomenon I call Protecting the Deal. Sometimes as you approach closing, everyone surrounding the seller starts talking about "what's best for the deal." The reality is that a lot of people's prosperity is riding on a successful sale. Your employees only get their big Payday if the sale happens. Some consultants only pocket their enormous fees if the deal closes. Certainly buyers only succeed if they actually buy your business. The lenders, settlement companies, and even caterers only celebrate when the final wire transfers are made at closing. The bank accounts of a whole mob of people are riding on you not getting in the way of the deal. They will subtly—and not so subtly—let you know that getting the deal done is more important than any one person.

Wrong.

You're not Spock sacrificing his life on *Star Trek* because the needs of the many outweigh the needs of the few. This is all about business, not world peace. You're the founder. As I recall, you're the one with the blood blisters from putting your nose to the grindstone. Do the right thing. Protect your team—and yourself.

# 34

## The Documents

### *Praying over Commas*

Forget those headlines about handshake deals or agreements written on the back of a napkin. The guys who used to operate that way won't be eligible for parole for years. Count on your sale—when and if it closes—going Old School. The paperwork will be "you gotta be kidding me" long—literally hundreds of mind-boggling pages.

The good thing is, you don't need to read any of it. That's not your job. That's what your advisors get the big bucks for. It's their job. Your responsibility is to hear them out, make good decisions about what points to fight for and what issues to concede—and then support them when they do battle to protect you. Make sure your team doesn't go overboard. Rein in any overly enthusiastic detail nuts, brush the leaves off their shoulders, and point out the forest.

Sometimes, though, you're the one who isn't careful. You might be terrified of losing the deal. Or you're just worn-out, impatient, and sick of it all. You'll do anything to get the deal done. Or maybe you think the buyer is wonderful, the contract is "standard," and your people are being nervous Nellies. So you shrug off dire warnings from your advisors and sign anything the buyer wants.

I've seen it happen. You are having all kinds of warm and fuzzy meetings with the buyer. Love is in the air. Everyone is talking about the importance of trust and values and relationships. The buyers seem like great people, the best you've ever met. They get you. You get them.

You're clicking. They want to keep you on after the sale. They see you helping drive your old business to new heights with your wisdom and experience and their money and connections. The deal documents seem like an insignificant sideshow—an irrelevancy managed by people who don't get it.

Watch out. Don't get fooled. Once the sale closes, these conference room romances almost always vanish. You and the buyers drift apart. They don't call and stop returning your calls. Where did the love go?

Then something bad happens. Someone sues your old company. Or sales plunge when a big customer walks away from a contract. Or your old protégées go crazy-over-budget on a project and profits nosedive. Your ex-BFFs, the buyers, haul the contract out of storage and hunt down a clause that says you're responsible. Now they want you to start signing again. But this time they want you signing checks—your own personal ones, that is—and it looks like it's gonna cost you a bundle.

Whoops.

It's too late to get cautious now.

## "Praying over Commas" Redux

All you have to do is lob one disaster grenade in that tranquil post-closing world and next thing you know everyone is pointing fingers, poring over documents, and looking for swords and shields. I call it praying over commas.

Folks who couldn't care less about the documents before the deal closed are suddenly studying every speck of ink on the page and proposing harebrained defenses. I get these wacky theories all the time and it's hard to answer them with a straight face:

> **YES:** a contract is valid if you sign it one day and the buyer signs the next day.

> **NO:** signing a contract in a red ink does not invalidate the contract.

**YES:** a contract is still enforceable if some of the sheets don't have page numbers.

**NO:** it's not duress if you agreed to something because you really wanted the money.

Buyers pay their lawyers a lot of money to make those documents binding. Barring a miracle, once the deal is closed it's too late—too late to improve the deal and too late to change the deal. Yes, sometimes you find a way out of the mess or enough ammo to force a compromise on the buyer. But you're lucky to get half as good a result as you would've with the right measures in advance.

Either protect against risk when you can—when you're still negotiating the documents—or accept the consequences. The way to avoid praying over commas is simple: be careful when it counts.

## The Kitchen Sink

Don't be surprised if you get a mountain of documents from the buyer. The purchase agreement alone can run a hundred pages. And that's just one document. The whole craziness can easily include ten to twenty different agreements—everything from that massive purchase agreement, to a noncompete agreement for you, to new employment agreements for your executive team.

Buyers want protection. Face it: they're shelling out a lot of money—and they don't want to lose it. One type of buyer tackles this risk with deal documents that require you to make thousands of promises and hundreds of guarantees. In a twisted sense, they trust you. That is, they'll rely on your word that you'll deliver. Other buyers won't take that chance—they want to personally check everything. They perform due diligence that feels like they're inspecting everything from your first-grade report card, to your cable-video bills, to your clothes hamper. Worse, nowadays most buyers have you make all those promises and they still don't trust you. They require both insanely onerous deal documents and intense due diligence—and they don't leave out the kitchen sink.

Whatever. You're not going to read all of these documents anyway. So here are the *CliffsNotes*. This paperwork accomplishes about a half a dozen things:

**REPRESENTATIONS AND WARRANTIES:** You have to swear there is no bad stuff concerning your business. You've paid your taxes, you didn't sleep with your assistant and then fire him, and you haven't bribed any foreign princes to get contracts.

**COVENANTS:** You promise to do good things and not do bad things. For example, you will continue to work with them for a year and you won't compete with them for three more.

**TRANSFERS:** You agree to sell your assets or stock. Ta-da! Here it is. You're selling the business. Make sure to spell out that you keep the original LeRoy Neiman of Tiger—or whatever else you want.

**TAXES:** You and the buyer divvy up the taxes. First, the tax gurus tote it up. Second, the attorneys whack it up. Third, you pay your hunk.

**CONDITIONS AND CONTINGENCIES:** You usually agree that the buyer doesn't have to purchase your business unless certain things happen. They may be waiting on financing or governmental approvals.

**CLOSING:** You get the procedures for closing. It's going to be at the buyer's office, but they'll give you a heads-up as to the time and date.

**MISCELLANEOUS:** You get the "boilerplate" provisions. Mostly this says what state you sue each other in and who pays whose attorneys' fees. Exciting stuff!

That's it. Nothing real complicated—once you get past the first few hundred pages.

## Stranger in a Strange Land

You're the owner, not a lawyer, investment banker, or CPA. How do you handle all the documents? You don't.

You manage the process.

First, appoint a team leader who supervises the document review and negotiation. This is usually going to be your top lawyer but could be both your lawyer and investment banker as co-captains. Give the leader some jobs. Make sure the leader creates a schedule for the review and negotiation of documents, as well as the due-diligence process.

Second, have your team study the documents and identify the problems and issues. Your team leader should then survey the group and prepare a list of concerns. The list should include their analysis of the risks and suggested counterproposals.

Third, you should schedule regular meetings, usually once a week. Bad meetings can be a colossal waste of time. So have good ones. Always send out an agenda in advance. Set a firm start and stop time. Stick to the agenda and time frame unless you're truly dealing with a new development or emergency. Create action items—specific tasks or next steps, with deadlines—as a product of each meeting. Before you end a meeting, set your next meeting and what needs to be accomplished by then.

If you're not a "meeting person" or you're afraid of racking up outrageous fees with all those meetings, recognize that time kills deals. The longer a sale drags on, the more likely something will derail it. But if you've assembled the right deal team, you're working with successful, busy people who have a lot on their plates. Your deal is not their only project. By having meetings, you force your deal to the top of their priority list. No one wants to show up for one of these meetings and face the rest of the team without having done their homework. This peer pressure motivates people to get their assignments done on time. So have the damn meetings!

Fourth, be decisive. Gather whatever info you need. Take the time you need. Encourage debates among your team members. Then decide. Don't flip-flop. Don't make your team negotiate hard to get what you asked for and then ask them later to go back and get something different. Try that twice and your team will stop trying hard.

You've run a successful business. Now run a successful sale.

## All's Well That Ends Well

If your business continues to do well after the sale, the buyer rarely looks at the deal documents or comes after you. They're happy. They leave well enough alone.

Once you close, the buyer traditionally sends the documents off to a company that binds the agreements in beautiful leather-bound books with gold lettering. Increasingly, the buyers forgo that sacred ritual and instead convert the documents to PDFs and put them all on a disk. You get a CD-ROM in a plastic casing instead of something nice for your bookcase. In any event, the parties keep the documents handy for a while to make post-closing payments and adjustments. Unless something bad happens, rarely does anyone read these documents or even check to see if you're complying.

Also, bad stuff rarely pops up after a deal anymore because the due-diligence process has become so rigorous in the last few decades. Any skeletons likely got dragged out in front of you at a bargaining session—whereupon the buyer took an ax to the sales price. So bad news is almost always old news. Sure, sometimes a buyer sues a seller after the deal closes. If you lied, stole, or cheated and didn't get caught earlier, you may get a registered letter one day and have to spend a lot of time and money with your lawyers and theirs.

But normally, selling your business is like pledging a fraternity. The hazing is at the beginning. Then you get to party.

# 35

# **Due Diligence**

*The Business Version of a Cavity Search*

Usually if we're doing something important, especially if we're spending a lot of money, we investigate. We evaluate how well something works and we probe for problems. It's called due diligence. If you're buying a house, you may get an inspector to look behind the walls, in the attic, and under the floors. If you're shopping for a used car, you should see whether it is on a list of the autos that got flooded in Katrina. When you meet your significant other's family for the first time, I'll bet you check out how that gene pool is working. Due diligence is everywhere.

If you're lucky enough to get a good offer for the sale of your business, the buyer will want to turn over all the stones and thoroughly check you out. Typically buyers will give you a list of documents that they want, as well as a list of questions they want you to answer. These aren't short lists. Even if you give them a ton of information, they usually want more. They also send in experts to review your financial records, inspect your facilities, and interview your employees. Sometimes they want to talk to your customers. Occasionally they even want to quiz folks who used to work for you. Then they'll ask you for explanations about everything they just learned. When you think that you can't stand it anymore, they want more.

That's all normal. Most buyers don't part with their money until they're completely comfortable with your business. But if you're punching through cobwebs looking for old files, you've got to wonder why buyers are so obsessed. The truth is that for all their smarts, they've been burned in the past and now they're afraid. You get one surprise like that guy in *The Crying Game* and you tend to get really cautious. So the buying team is sitting around saying, "What are we missing? How can we get hurt?" They're afraid you're hiding stuff and they won't find about it until it's too late.

That makes due diligence a necessary evil for both sides. They've got to check you out before they'll do the deal. You've got to get through it to get the deal done. Don't get hung up on how much work it is or that you're miserable doing it. Treat it like an extreme endurance sport with a medal, cold beer, and an adoring crowd waiting for you at the finish line.

## Enough Is Enough

There are limits. Some due diligence is just plain counterproductive. A couple of buddies of mine ran a profitable business. They didn't know if they wanted to keep growing the business or just cash out. A competitor came along talking about buying them out for big dollars. He suggested my guys should also stay on as partial owners and lead a new division with the buyer. It was tempting and they all took it to the next step. Then the buyers' due-diligence team showed up—acting like storm troopers. They didn't burn down any houses or hang any villagers, but it felt like it. The due-diligence team insulted my buddies' management skills, criticized the way they kept records, and insinuated they were cooking the books to make the financials look better. The sellers realized they could never work with these buyers and called off the negotiations. The buyers were actually dumbfounded at the turn of events, which only confirmed that they were clueless and would have been terrible partners.

But bad behavior in due diligence cuts both ways. One seller I represented reminded me of my old dog. On a hot day my Lab would lie down in the middle of a walk and not budge. You couldn't drag him home (trust me). Likewise, in the middle of due diligence, this seller abruptly announced: "That's it! That's all they're getting from me. No more answers. No more documents." The buyer was a publicly traded company, so their due diligence was rigorous but not crazy. They asked for normal stuff—like contracts, customer lists, financial statements, and software licenses. I never figured out why the seller threw his tantrum. Perhaps he felt it was all too intrusive or too much work. Or he was hiding something. Maybe he was just a cranky old man. Despite my pleading, he didn't turn over so much as another lunch receipt. We barely kept the deal alive and got the business sold—but only by swallowing a 15 percent cut in the sales price. The buyer kept those boxes of records, but it cost him millions of dollars.

What is appropriate for the buyer to ask for? Well, virtually everything about your business. But don't fall into the trap of repeatedly giving them the same thing because they can't find the last copy you sent. And—except for legitimate follow-up questions—make them ask for everything all at once.

How should you handle due diligence?

## Open Wide

Due diligence is a little like feeding an infant. You're the infant. The more you struggle, the messier it's going to be. So cooperate.

Still, if you act like a doormat, people will walk all over you. So manage the process:

**ORGANIZE:** If your records look like a mess, the buyer will only want to dig deeper to check for skeletons in your closet. The bigger the mess, the worse their due diligence. Clean up your act—in advance.

**ANTICIPATE:** Figure out what the buyer will want and get it ready. Ask your investment banker and lawyer for sample due-diligence checklists. There is no question that the buyer will ask for information about your competitors and market, your management team and employees, your sales and marketing, and your facilities and operations and—above all else—financial information. They'll also want all of your "material" agreements, such as customer contracts, loan agreements, significant equipment and real estate leases, and supply or purchase contracts. If you're ready to provide the buyer with all of these necessary materials quickly, you reduce the potential for delays and repetitive requests.

**ESTABLISH A PROCESS:** Require that the buyer provide you with a complete list of what they want. The only add-ons should be legitimate follow-up. Also require a schedule for the process. Stick to it and insist that the buyer does, too.

**ACCOUNTABILITY:** Catalog everything you provide to the buyer. Make sure the buyer knows you're doing it. For example, always include a cover sheet that lists what you're providing. This makes it harder for the buyer to ask you for the same thing repeatedly—whether out of laziness or out of a desire to stall.

**PREPARE FOR PROBLEMS:** Did anyone else ever consider buying your business but walk away? What concerned them? Ask your deal team, especially the outsiders, what is likely to bother the buyer. If any of these concerns can be addressed by beefing up your due-diligence materials—or your company itself—fix it now. For example, you may not be producing enough financial reports or the right ones, or the ones you produce are full of errors. Correct that now, so when you hand your materials over to the buyer, they're impressed—not scared.

If you follow these rules you're going to limit the buyer's ability to stall or renegotiate. It improves your odds of getting the deal done and avoiding a reduction in the sales price.

## What's Good for the Goose

Sometimes you need to do your own due diligence. If you're being paid part of the sales price in a promissory note or stock—or if you're counting on the buyer to take on your old responsibilities after the deal—you're at risk. You need your own crime scene investigation—before the crime.

You may not realize it, but it's fairly common for the buyer to set up a worthless shell company to make the actual purchase. The real purchaser—the one with the deep pockets—only puts enough cash in that empty shell to close on the sale and fund a little bit of operating costs. If all goes well, they feed in more money. If not, they close up shop and walk away—leaving you empty-handed or, worse, still on the hook for your old business obligations. Obviously, this setup provides meager protection for you after closing. You need your own due diligence to ferret this out. Ask the tough questions. Then protect yourself. You might need airtight guarantees from the folks with the real money or a commitment to put more cash into the buyer. The bottom line is that you're also entitled to full disclosure—and the protection it yields.

## Remember the Big Picture

Due diligence is necessary for every good deal. People are entitled to know what they're buying into. But watch out for buyers who don't just want information. Some drag out the process or dredge up issues to wear down both you and the sales price. For them, due diligence is also a tactic. Don't fall for that. Manage the process. You'll profit from it.

# 36

# The Deal's ~~Done~~ Being Renegotiated

### *Beware the Retrade*

I was never supposed to get the e-mail. The buyer's attorney and I had been clashing over the terms of a sale. He was protecting his client. I was fighting for mine. I thought the negotiations were spirited but not mean-spirited. I was wrong. That became abundantly clear when the buyer's CFO screwed up and sent me an e-mail meant for his own attorney. "Just tell them we'll sign the letter of intent," it revealed. "When we have them tied up, we'll renegotiate. Once the other buyers are gone, the seller will have to take a lower price."

Some buyers make an art of the "retrade." They sign up for a deal that they don't intend to honor, drag the seller along through due diligence and documentation, and wear him or her down. Then they renegotiate for a lower price. One guy I know lost $25 million on a retrade.

There, you've been warned.

## Scratch 'N' Dent

Like the CFO who sent me that revealing e-mail, some buyers intend to retrade from the very beginning. It's the way they do business. Their business model depends on getting bargain prices for acquisitions, and they take great pride in pinning you down and squeezing you for a discount.

Other buyers don't plan on retrading. But they'll take advantage of an opportunity when they see one. You have to fight both types.

The typical retrade works like this. In your letter of LOI, you agree to a formula that assumes a certain level of future sales or profits and yields the agreed sales price. Then you lose a big customer or go way over budget on a project. Your revenues or earnings drop. Next thing you know, the buyer is stomping around the conference room and throwing a fake fit. He waves the LOI around in the air, shrieking that he's entitled to a lower sales price. It's all very dramatic.

Sometimes a retrade isn't aimed at your sales price. Instead they blast other key deal terms. For example, you bargained for an all-cash deal. You're supposed to get a wire transfer at closing and then you never have to look at these jerks again—except at The Club. But then the buyer's Board of Directors insists you take part of the sales price in a promissory note. Worse, because the buyer's lender will have a mortgage on everything, your loan will be unsecured. If the buyer runs out of money, you don't get paid.

How does this happen? Why would any seller put up with this?

Retrading works for several reasons. First, if a buyer walks away from your deal, you're stigmatized. It's like wearing a scarlet letter. Other purchasers assume that something is wrong with your business and you're damaged goods. If they're willing to deal with you at all, they'll demand a fire-sale price.

Second, you already kissed off the other potential purchasers who had the hots for your business. When you picked one buyer, the others got over you and moved on. By now, they're probably dating other businesses.

Third, after haggling with one buyer, you're worn-out and distracted—maybe even desperate. You used up a ton of energy and charm presenting your business to a lot of suitors. Then you spent heaps of time and buckets of money on your outside advisors. You negotiated "the deal"—or so you thought—until those barbarians bailed on you. You're not exactly fresh and ready for another fifteen-round boxing match.

## Prevention Is the Key

This is another situation where avoiding the problem in the first place is a kajillion times better than trying to solve it afterward. So here are some safe-dating tips:

**SCREEN THE BUYERS:** If you have assembled the right deal team, one of the best things they can do is help you avoid the wrong buyer. Now is the time to be your most vigilant—while you still have the option of selling to someone else. Don't rush and don't be pushed. Before you commit to exclusive negotiations with one buyer, don't assume anything. Check out the following:

- *History.* Does the buyer have a history of retrading? Your investment banker should know or find out. Ideally, you want buyers that regularly purchase other businesses and won't dare jeopardize their reputations among the investment-banking community by retrading deals. They don't want to repel sellers because they're known for unfairly retrading.

- *Financing.* Always try to pick a buyer that has locked up financing. Some purchasers strike a bargain with you before they arrange financing for the deal. When that happens, the buyer might retrade your deal later to satisfy their lender. Some even use financing requirements as a ploy to renegotiate.

- *Authority.* Confirm that the buyer has the authorization to do your deal. Some purchasers will negotiate all of the sale terms with you. Then they reveal that they can't proceed until they have the approval of their Board of Directors, a joint-venture partner, or their investment committee. By then, you've already put your best deal on the table and now they want you to sweeten the pot. Hello, retrade. I call this scam "second-level negotiating." You're negotiating with the first level, but the second level makes the ultimate decisions. Avoid this setup early on by nailing down and negotiating only with the deal makers. When that isn't practical, don't commit to exclusive negotiations until that second level has approved the major deal terms.

**AVOID ROOKIE MISTAKES:** First-time sellers often make a bunch of rookie mistakes that increase the odds of a retrade. Here's how to avoid some of the classic errors:

- *Don't Overcommit.* Don't lock yourself up in exclusive negotiations for too long. Insist that you're free to walk away or bargain with others if you haven't agreed on all of the major deal terms within ninety days.

- *Don't Procrastinate.* Don't leave important issues for later. For instance, if you're happy to sell, but you refuse to agree to a noncompete restriction, get it out on the table early.

- *Don't Overpromise.* Don't provide the buyer with overly optimistic forecasts of future revenues or profits. Plenty of buyers drag out the deal for far longer than you would ever expect. If your estimates prove to be inflated, they'll hit you over the head with your own spreadsheet and demand a lower sales price.

- *Don't Sell in a Bad Market.* If you try to sell in a bad market, you're fighting uphill the whole time. This may seem obvious, but you wouldn't believe how many sellers ignore it. Just because you're sick of the business doesn't mean it's a good time to unload it. Instead, wait until buyers are in a frenzy and are more afraid of losing deals than getting a better one.

## The Retrade

Despite all of your precautions, you still may get hit with a retrade. What should you do?

### Evaluate Your Options

Honestly and objectively evaluate your options. If you're fortunate, you've kept your business running smoothly, you have plenty of cash coming in, and you don't feel pressured to sell. However, if you took your eye off the ball and let the wheels come off your business, it may be tempting to sell and move on. Can you? Have all of the other buyers moved on? Are you tied up by an exclusive negotiating clause that binds you to the retrader?

### Determine If the Retrader Is Serious

Plenty of buyers will try a retrade but don't want to lose a deal over it. Given the choice—and perhaps an opportunity to save face—these buyers will still buy on terms close to the original bargain. How do you know? There are some telltale clues:

- Are they saying no but acting yes? A buyer that is serious and committed to the retrade stops working on the deal. They don't continue due diligence or document negotiation. The committed retrader freezes everything until you surrender.

- Do they say they aren't interested but still call you? It's "the phone call rule." If you're still in their Friends & Family plan, even though they've given you an ultimatum, they want the deal. They're not likely to walk away to get a lower price.

- But when they're adamant about getting a better deal, they move on quickly if you say no. They don't pester you. They don't return your calls. They're gone, baby, gone.

## The Walk-Away

Do you feel lucky?

When you are faced with a retrade, the high-stakes response is the "walk-away"—big risk, potentially big reward. Tell the buyer no and show them the door. But only do this if you've got to get your price.

If the buyer wants a bargain and you aren't willing to give it to them, you aren't losing anything. It's inevitable the deal will fall apart. Go back to running your business. Fix what's broken with your company, take a breather, and get ready for the next buyer.

If that retrader really wants your business, they'll come back. You'll get your price. Go ahead; make your day.

# 37

## Dead Deals

*Picking Up the Pieces*

It's over. Stuff happens. Deals die. Boo-hoo.

Deals crater for a variety of reasons. Some have nothing to do with you. Buyers change their minds abruptly and go in a different direction. One wants something sexy for its investors and inexplicably concludes that your new, nonpolluting 200 miles per gallon sports car isn't appealing. Another loses their financing and can't find the dough to close. Still others encounter problems with their existing acquisitions and need to devote all their time and resources to keeping those businesses alive.

Other times, it is all about you. The buyer feels too much competition is about to enter your market or worries the government intends to hammer your industry with regulations that could vaporize profits. Or it dawns on all involved that there is a massive culture clash between your organization and the buyer's people. Whatever the reason—or excuse—deals die all of the time.

But remember that you didn't get this far because you suck. You built a substantial business. You attracted a buyer that spent a lot of time and effort trying to make a deal work. Just because you didn't cross the finish line doesn't mean you haven't been running a great race. Plenty of businesses don't sell on the first try—or even the next few. This is no time to take up professional moping. Get back to work.

In business—as in life—it is not a question of whether bad things will happen to you. It's all about how you react. Pick yourself up. Learn from what went wrong. In each dead deal, there are lessons. Some lessons are as simple as avoiding certain buyers in the future. Stay away from the ones that aren't serious, don't have the financing or team to make the deal happen, or don't have the values and integrity to get a fair deal done.

But, certainly, sometimes you've got flaws in your business. If you don't want to repeat this painful episode, learn from it. Look in the mirror. You may be part of the problem. Then ask your team what went wrong—and try not to look like you're in a firing mood. It is also critical to get your investment banker to prepare a report analyzing the reasons the deal died, how your company contributed to the problems, and what should be done to fix them. This next one is a stretch. If possible, interview the buyer and ask their team what's wrong with your business and what you should change. Most folks will sugarcoat any criticism, so let your outside advisors do the questioning and have them ask for the painful truth.

Don't be defensive. Of course, that's easier said than done. But if you listen to the diagnosis, you'll know what medicine you need.

## Work, Work, Work

Now devise a plan to fix those problems and get to work. You may need to upgrade members of your team. The buyer may have found a real drop-off between you and the next person down on the org chart. Maybe your financial systems aren't robust enough—time to replace the abacus! Or competitors are starting to eat your lunch. Whatever the problems, you need to tackle these issues to sell—or even survive.

You may not be up for the challenge. You may still be bummed out about that whole dead-deal thing. No mansion. No millions. No hot young bodies surrounding you by the pool (come on, really, that last one was never going to happen, deal or no deal). But that's all history—for now. So, sure, be sad. Don't shave or change your underwear. Eat comfort food. Stay in bed and watch *When Harry Met Sally*—again. Take the whole damn weekend off.

But then get back in your office bright and early Monday morning with an espresso in one fist and a Red Bull in the other and your executive team fired up.

Because that's how you roll.

# 38

## Last-Minute Surprises

### *What the Hell!?*

I am at my desk right now having delivered the news to opposing counsel that the world has changed and so has a deal. As I write, the ground is moving under financial institutions throughout the world. Banks aren't lending, companies are failing, and tent cities are popping up across the country. This has filtered down to a mega-deal that I am negotiating. The other side dragged out the deal and asked for one too many things. My clients just decided that they won't give in and, worse, all the scary headlines have them questioning whether to do the deal at all. The other side needs to scale back and make some concessions or the deal is off. Times have changed—suddenly.

Great depressions don't happen every day, but last-minute surprises do. They can come at you from every angle:

**FINANCING:** This is a regular heart-stopper. Like Mark Twain said, a banker is a fellow that lends you his umbrella when the sun is shining but wants it back at the first sign of rain. I don't care how many high fives a buyer gets from his loan officer on the fairway, a goodly percent of all eleventh-hour glitches involve money and lenders. The interest rate or collateral requirements go up; the amount available goes down. Any of it can hurt or kill the deal.

**LOST CONTRACTS:** You've had a contract with the government for years. It's your most reliable moneymaker. The client loves you and has never expressed a concern. Sure, they make you go through a competition every few years to keep it, but you always win. If there ever was a lock, this is it. Then a month before closing, "Old Faithful" dries up. There goes a chunk of your revenues and now the buyer has cold feet.

**DISSENT:** Someone in the chain of command says no to the deal. We had one sale where the President—who owned 50 percent of the company—supervised the negotiations of the sale over a span of months. Surprise! His crazy, intransigent partner decided to boycott for a better deal—two days before the closing.

**APPROVALS:** One sale required the assignment of a couple of dozen leases for office and lab facilities across the country. The seller had wisely negotiated provisions in most of the leases that would allow the buyer to take over each lease—without landlord consent—if the company was sold. But a few of the really old leases required approval of the transfer by the landlord. Those few agreements put a nine-figure deal at the mercy of some sketchy landlords who wanted to squeeze money and favors out of the seller in exchange for their okay. Not exactly the send-off the seller was hoping for.

**BIG BROTHER:** One client was buying out a competitor whose owner was moving into a high-level government position. The deal required ethics approval from a government agency. Unfortunately, these bureaucrats had a sundial in their courtyard that they used to speed them through the approval process. After months of delays, the G-men finally sent a list of unrealistic demands that almost torpedoed the sale. Luckily, but not quickly, we were able to talk them out of the worst requirements and massage the rest into something manageable.

How's a worn-out, bedraggled seller supposed to handle that last roundhouse punch in the face? Above all else, don't freak out. You need to roll with each of those hits. Be flexible.

You may be itching for a fight, but now's not the time. Instead get creative. Bridge the gap. If you've gotten this far, you have a good team. Task them with finding answers and compromises. Give the buyer a menu of choices or one or two brilliant solutions.

Depending on what ails you, you may have to do one or more of the following:

- *Reduce the sales price—or take part of it in a note or stock in the buyer.* This hurts, but once you pull off the Band-Aid, you're done.

- *Use a "hold-back" or escrow of part of the sale price.* This is employed more often than you'd like. The money is held to compensate the buyer if any of the dark storm clouds actually burst. If the danger passes, you get the money. It's risky, though, because with a stack of cash sitting there it's tempting for the buyer to "find" bad stuff.

- *Put up a guarantee.* The buyer makes you sign a contract where you guarantee the deal or some key issue—like hitting certain sales or profit targets. Sometimes just the fact that you're willing to make this commitment reassures the buyer. They never follow up and enforce your obligation. Other times the buyer is dead serious and makes you pay for the slightest default. It can cost you.

- *Pair one of these last-minute concessions with an "earn-out."* If the company does well, you get more. Maybe you had to cough up a guarantee or discount the price. But then if sales soar, you get a bonus. If they forget to offer it, don't forget to ask.

- *Avoid the buyer postponing closing to see what happens.* Here you're locked into the deal, but they can walk away. When you delay a deal, it's often worse than killing it. You're trapped—locked into a sale with no certainty it will get done. Your employees are in limbo and some may move on to more stable environs. Clients may also wander away. You're at the buyer's mercy. It's like when my older brother used to pin me down with his knees on my arms and dangle spit over my face. Again, stay away from this one.

If the world changed on you, accept it quickly. Don't hold on to what might have been. Denial kills tons of deals—and wealth. Of course, we all want to make a deal that makes us happy. But sometimes we need to quickly revisit what makes us happy—in order to make the deal.

# 39

## The Closing

*Great Expectations*

Some closings are disasters. I survived one where the buyer came to the table itching for a fight—and a lower price. He stormed into the conference room chomping on an unlit cigar and tore into the doe-eyed seller. The buyer hurled rapid-fire accusations and demanded a huge price reduction, his face reddening as he worked himself up into a frenzy. The stunned seller finally unfroze and fought back. What started out as enhanced interrogation became a "hide the china" screaming match. People said stuff they could never take back. The next time the parties saw each other they were in a courtroom flanked by attorneys. Not pretty. That's one deal that never closed.

But that was a commercial real estate deal—where some insiders think you're lazy or incompetent if you don't go full-Khrushchev and bang your shoe on the conference table to get a discount at the closing.

Don't worry. None of that brawling happens when you're closing on the sale of your company. Closing on a business sale is all polite protocol, like those refined bows when heads of state meet. The worst thing that will happen at your closing is the host runs out of toner and someone has to run over to Staples. Everyone might sit around breaking the tension with lame jokes about the bank failing before you get your money. Ha-freakin'-ha.

So what's the procedure? What exactly do you do? All is answered in what I call The Three Ceremonies.

## Ceremony #1: The Signing

The closing takes place at the office of the buyer or their attorneys. In recent years, some closings have been virtual—accomplished merely with the exchange of signature pages by FedEx or e-mail. But in deals of about $20 million or more, people want a live, let's-all-hold-hands ceremony.

Some of these closings are pretty glitzy—using fancy pens engraved with the names of the buyer and seller, cameras flashing, and even a videographer capturing the show. But mostly, you sign a lot. In every closing, there are stacks of documents on the conference table and people insisting you sign dozens of pages and maybe even put your initials on a few hundred more—all in blue ink, so they can tell originals from copies. No, you don't have to read any of it. Your attorneys did that earlier. The lawyers just need to check and make sure you're signing the final version of everything, not some outdated draft. Also, don't forget your driver's license. Even though you're the main attraction, you still may need to document your identity for the notary.

Now sit down for this. Even though you're signing away your company, you won't be getting a check at the closing. First, they don't even use checks anymore—paper is oh so passé. Instead the buyer wires the money into your bank account. But they're not going to send you the money right away. The attorneys for the buyer need to confirm a bunch of things before you get paid, like the transfer of title to assets. Most likely, you'll get your money a day or two after closing. In the meantime, stay out of the way of buses. Strangely enough, some of your consultants will probably get their fees on closing day. It's just how this business works.

## Ceremony #2: The Celebration

Next, there is a celebration dinner at a fancy restaurant. Your investment banker often plays host and pays for it. But like the bride's father paying for the wedding, that's not a law.

The festivities are lavish, open-bar, catered, let-off-steam, joke-filled, warmhearted affairs. The two sworn enemies have come together as one. It's like the sci-fi movie where previously warring Earthlings put aside centuries of bloodthirsty revenge and band together to battle the alien invaders. Who knew we had so much in common?

You should have gifts ready to hand out to your deal team. They don't have to be fancy. It's completely up to you. I've seen everything from Montblanc pen sets, to brass desk clocks to pricey watches. It all depends on the size of the deal, the value your team added, and—most of all—your affection for the participants. In extraordinary cases, where someone has been with you for a very long time or added tremendous value to the deal, you may want to privately give a bonus. None of this is required. Presumably, they're already getting handsomely rewarded for their contributions to the company. This is about your heart, not your wallet.

You should also give a speech at the dinner thanking your deal team and the buyer. Try to single out everyone on your team for individual recognition. Often this speech and the gift giving go together. You may be shy about giving this speech. Some people are more afraid of public speaking than anything else—including dying. At a funeral, they'd rather be in the casket than giving the eulogy. If that's you, pick someone from your team to make this presentation. It's common and completely acceptable. Regardless of who speaks, you don't want to miss what may be your last opportunity to publicly thank those who helped you achieve so much.

## Ceremony #3: It's Midnight, Oh-My-God-What-Have-I-Done!?

After the celebration ends, this final "ceremony" begins. Sometimes it hits you while you're still sipping your closing-dinner Champagne. Other times it takes days or weeks. Inevitably though, and seemingly out of nowhere, you'll be overwhelmed with a creepy, weird emptiness. Till now, the sale has been all theory. Now it's reality. Your company is no longer yours. You spent years building it. It became your home away from home. For some, it became their home instead of home. It's all gone now, like your only child went off to college—on Mars.

"Did I just make the biggest mistake of my life?" you wonder. "After all, money isn't everything." These feelings overcome virtually every person who ever sells a business.

Life goes on. You'll see. There is another chapter.

# 40

# Now What?

*Who Am I? And What Am I Doing Here?*

Surprisingly, the euphoria doesn't last long.

You should be proud. You built and sold your business for a fortune. Not many people have achieved this. You didn't inherit this. You put in a lot of time and effort. It took great tenacity, but you persevered and succeeded. You grew as a person. You gave a livelihood to others, mentored them, and improved the quality of their lives. You achieved financial security for your family. Maybe you even made the world a better place. But if you think success is going to melt away all of life's problems, you're wrong.

You still have to watch out for a few potholes.

## Money, Money, Money

Money isn't the root of all evil. But it certainly stirs up a lot of problems. Try to avoid the worst:

**NO IMPULSE CONTROL:** The cash you got from the sale of your business isn't government "stimulus" money. Don't throw it around like it's burning a hole in your pocket. Some successful entrepreneurs waste their wealth. They're like lottery ticket winners who don't really feel they earned the money—cuz, duh, they didn't. So they go out and throw it around. They "invest" their money in limos with hot tubs and things that make your car bounce up and down. You're smarter than that. You just need some impulse control. Splurge on one or two luxuries so you can get the craziness out of your system and then lock up the rest of your money.

**PUBLIC DISPLAYS OF WEALTH:** At the other extreme, some people feel so guilty about their newfound wealth, they're loath to spend any of it. They're especially self-conscious about buying anything that others might frown upon. They feel they don't deserve to treat themselves. A good solution is to pretend a friend has come to you for advice. Your buddy is in the exact same situation as you. Should he or she get that new car or vacation home? If you're giving advice to a hypothetical friend, you're more objective. You might overcome feelings of guilt that prevent you from buying something you've always wanted, especially when it doesn't hurt your financial security.

**MONEY MISMANAGEMENT:** Get guidance from financial advisors. But don't turn over control—or your trust—to them. I hate to break bad news. Even with all of that money you got from selling your business, you can't completely retire. You need to manage your finances for the rest of your life. That doesn't mean studying technical stock charts or analyzing soil reports for real estate investments. But stay informed and make all of the big decisions.

## The Out-of-Work Blues

Virtually every successful entrepreneur who sells a business is going to feel a loss of identity. You were the leader of a business. Every time you walked into a room, people said things like "He runs XYZ Corp.," "She owns the fastest-growing business around," or "You have to meet her; she's a real go-getter in the business community." Now what?

You're unemployed.

Before you sold, you were your business. You identified who you were with what you did. When people asked about you, you talked about your job or your business. Now what do you say? What do you even put on your name tag: "Ex–Important Person" or "Used to Have a Purpose in Life"?

You're going to be lost for a while. You can't go from sixty-hour weeks juggling a dozen plates to game shows on television, golf, and naps without some kind of disorientation. You were wrapped up in what you did. Now you don't do it anymore. If the feelings of loss are strong, see a shrink. Talk it out. Also, hang out with other former entrepreneurs who got past this stage and found new, healthy ways to enjoy themselves. They can be role models for your next act in life.

Business success is wonderful. But it doesn't always provide all of the meaning or fulfillment we crave. Step back and assess what you want the rest of your life to be about. You may want to swim across the English Channel, mentor inner-city youths, or take up painting. Take a deep breath, exhale, and think about what you want to do next. You've got the time and money now. Get going.

## Honey, I'm Home

You've been at work a lot. Don't be shocked if your significant other learned to live quite nicely without you around all the time. He or she is likely to be a bit uncomfortable if you plop back, full-time, into his or her gig. Go slow. Don't smother. Talk about the situation. Ask what he or she thinks would be good for the both of you. Face it, you may not have asked for his or her opinion about a lot of major things in the last few decades. It's time to start.

Likewise, you may be a stranger to your kids. Fix that. Show interest in their lives. But don't be a robot. Think about what's important to them—ask if you don't know—and reach out in a way that's meaningful to them. If you show sincere interest in their lives, they might just want to rebuild a relationship with you.

## Doubling Down—Don't

You didn't build your business or sell it in a day—and you certainly didn't do any of it without risk. But now you've earned some financial security. Don't jeopardize it. Don't dive into a new business without thinking things through carefully. Limit your investment and any personal guarantees. It is far more important to have a smaller role in a new venture than it is to gamble for greater wealth—at the risk of losing everything you've got.

Despite your past success, you can't count on duplicating it. You may achieve many more victories. Just don't bet on it.

You've finished a long, perilous, stressful, exciting, and rewarding journey that only a small percentage of entrepreneurs successfully complete. You've accomplished a lot and have so much to live for. Congratulations.

Be safe. Be happy.

# Index